NEW YEATS PAPERS IX

ROBERT O'DRISCOLL

SYMBOLISM AND SOME IMPLICATIONS OF THE SYMBOLIC APPROACH: W. B. YEATS DURING THE EIGHTEEN-NINETIES

THE DOLMEN PRESS

CONTENTS

I	The Nature of Symbolism	page 9
II	Twilight and the Rose: *The Celtic Twilight, The Secret Rose*, and *Stories of Red Hanrahan*	19
III	From Dream to Vision: *Rosa Alchemica, The Tables of the Law*, and *The Adoration of the Magi*	37
IV	Some Implications of the Symbolic Approach: *The Wind Among the Reeds*	48
V	A Beast and a Unicorn: *Where There is Nothing* and *The Unicorn from the Stars*	62

Epilogue 75

Notes on the text 77

General Editor: Liam Miller

© Robert O'Driscoll 1975
ISBN 0 85105 270 3

PR
5908
.S59
O3

Printed and published in the Republic of Ireland at the Dolmen Press, North Richmond Industrial Estate, North Richmond Street, Dublin 1. First published 1975.
Distributed outside Ireland, except in the United States of America and in Canada, by Oxford University Press.
Distributed in the United States of America and in Canada by Humanities Press Inc., 171 First Avenue, Atlantic Highlands, N.J. 07716.

PREFACE

This study traces the development and completion of one phase of Yeats's thought. At the beginning of the eighteen-nineties, in his commentary on Blake and in *Ideas of Good and Evil*, Yeats rejects the materialistic approach to experience and argues that man and the material world must be regarded as symbols, as expressions or embodiments of a spiritual mood rather than as complete in themselves. *The Celtic Twilight* traces Yeats's attempt to find in folk literature and life, in places where the traditional order of life remains unbroken, an approach to experience that contravenes the modern materialistic approach. *The Secret Rose* deals with the war between the spiritual and material world; *Stories of Red Hanrahan* with the separation of the two worlds; and *Rosa Alchemica*, *The Tables of the Law*, and *The Adoration of the Magi* with the apocalyptic annunciation of a new dispensation. *The Wind Among the Reeds* takes the poet beyond the threshold of symbolic apocalypse as, interested only in spiritual essences, he calls for the destruction of the material forms which, paradoxically, embody the essence he desires. *Where There is Nothing* carries the thought of *The Wind Among the Reeds* to its point of disintegration, and *The Unicorn from the Stars* was designed, in Yeats's words, 'to carry to a more complete realization the central idea of the stories of *The Secret Rose*.'

In this study I have not explored the influences on Yeats's work during the eighteen-nineties, but I have concentrated on presenting the primary levels of meaning in works which have to this point in time received little critical attention.

I am deeply grateful to the Canada Council for Research Grants which enabled me to complete this study.

Althea Gyles: Design from the back cover of the binding of
The Secret Rose, London 1897.

for
Lorna Reynolds
for courage in dark days
and gaiety in bright ones

I THE NATURE OF SYMBOLISM

I

To assume that Yeats acquired his knowledge of symbolism from Arthur Symons and the French *symbolistes* is no longer possible. It seems clear now that he found in *symboliste* theory and practice only the corroboration for discoveries he had already made in his study of Blake and the occult. Yeats himself was explicit on this point. In 1934 he wrote to Maurice Bowra:

> I don't think I was really much influenced by French Symbolists. My development was different, but that development was of such a nature that I felt I could not explain it, or even that it might make everybody hostile. When Symons talked to me about the Symbolistes, or read me passages from his translations from Mallarmé, I seized upon everything that at all resembled my own thought; here at last was something I could talk about. My symbolism came from actual experiments in vision, made by my friends or myself, in the society which called itself "The Hermetic Students", and continually talked over by myself and my friends. I felt that these investigations were private, and felt also, and indeed still feel, that one can only explain oneself if one draws one's illustrations from accepted schools of thought. Furthermore, I felt, that unaccepted schools, however profound, are incomplete because isolated from the rest of knowledge.[1]

Twenty years earlier he had written to Ernest Boyd:

> My interest in mystic symbolism did not come from Arthur Symons or any other contemporary writer. I have been a student of the medieval mystics since 1887.... My chief mystical authorities have been Boehme, Blake, and Swedenborg.
>   Of the French symbolists I have never had any detailed or accurate knowledge.[2]

In 1910, in an unpublished lecture on Symons and the Rhymers' Club, Yeats stated: 'what brought them to the same mind as myself, *by a different path*, was largely French influences.'[3] Earlier, in 1896, he argued that the French *symboliste* movement had 'no sufficient philosophy and criticism, . . . but if it cared it might find enough of both philosophy and criticism in the writings of William Blake to protect it from its opponents, and . . . from its own mistakes.' Some consistent philosophy of symbolism may, he posits, be 'hidden in the writings of M. Mallarmé', but these writings, he admits, he does not have 'French enough to understand'.[4] It is to Yeats's writings on William Blake then, and not to French *symboliste* theory and practice, that we must turn if we are interested in exploring his conception of symbolism.[5]

The most significant section of the three-volume edition and commentary on Blake which Yeats wrote with Edwin Ellis in the early eighteen-nineties is 'The Symbolic System', and the manuscripts of the work which survive establish that this section was almost completely written by Yeats.[6] But although the work was not published until 1893 Yeats had completed most of the section by the summer of 1891,[7] before he had much contact with either Arthur Symons or the *symboliste* movement.

In the beginning of all important things 'there is a moment when we understand more perfectly than we understand again until all is finished.'[8] 'The Symbolic System' and the other essays Yeats wrote during the eighteen-nineties present his clearest definition of symbolism and one of the clearest distinctions he was ever to make between the symbolic and materialist approach to experience. In these writings he shows that what the symbolist and materialist seek, the methods they use to discover it, and the way in which they express it, differ.

II

The materialist, Yeats argues, believes that the mind is 'actually one with the physical organism',[9] that there is no essential difference between the natural and spiritual order. Knowledge, the materialist believes, can be discovered through observation of the external world and the analysis of impressions derived from the five senses. The symbolist, on the other hand, begins by positing the 'absolute difference' between the natural and spiritual order: he regards the world as the external expression of what lies hidden in the mind of each individual. Consequently the symbolist does not reason from outer to inner, from effect to cause, but from prior to posterior, from cause to effect; he proceeds from intuition to concrete manifestation. The activity of the mind, he argues, must parallel the activity of the senses: indeed to him observation, sensation, and the external world are merely the means by which the inner world of the mind is revealed, 'the symbols or correspondence whereby the intellectual nature realizes or grows conscious of itself in detail.'[10] To the symbolist external nature is the shadow, not the substance, the distorted mirror of reality, not the reality itself.

The argument, however, grows more complicated. To the symbolist natural manifestations are seen as the way in which the intellectual nature becomes conscious of itself, but intellectual activity in turn is seen as the way in which the emotional finds expression. There are thus three great principles operating in the universe: the emotional, the intellectual, and the natural (the respective symbols of which are fire, air, and water). Of these the emotional principle is the highest.[11] The progression is from highest to lowest. All life, all art begins in a 'bodiless mood,' becomes then a 'surging thought,' and last 'a thing.'[12] The thing, the physical manifestation or action, is significant only in so far as it is the expression of a thought or emotion. At the centre of the universe, possessing neither 'form nor substance', is the 'universal mood' which Yeats calls God, the 'truth self-existing in its own essence.'[13] All intellectual and physical forms, all art and nature, the universe itself, are seen by the symbolist as expressions or embodiments of this universal mood. Art, therefore, is not an imitation or extension of nature, but uses the external world as a symbol 'to express subjective moods.'[14]

Materialism contracts man's consciousness by limiting him to personal experience; and, confined to the natural world, he must suffer the fate of all natural things, death. But if nature is regarded as a symbol, rather than as an entity complete in itself, death holds no power over the individual, for he realizes that only the natural body dies, that the spirit lives on in the symbols it creates. When history and the material world are regarded symbolically, as providing the metaphors and examples for the inspired intuitions of the mind, man is able to look beyond accidental forms, beyond the laws of nature and necessity, to the essence that these forms embody; he can pass beyond the particular experiences of the body, perception and memory, and see all things 'as with the eyes of God.' He can become a medium for universal emotion and enter into the 'one great mind or imagination, "the body of God." '

> We enter into this Divine body by the symbolism of things, as we enter into the world about us by perception of things, apart from their symbols, and by association of ideas in the memory—mystical trances come from leaving behind the last two faculties, and entering wholly into the world of symbolic perception of universal truths. The perception of the senses apart from symbol, limits us down to the narrow circle of personal experience, while association of ideas is essentially "spectral," coming as it does, not from perception of something apart from ourselves, but from the memory of sensations which get their peculiar value from being connected with our personal and "spectral" life. By symbolism we enter the universality of God, by sensation and the memory of sensation, we enter the world of Satan, which is "all nothing." [15]

In his writings during the eighteen-nineties Yeats makes a further differentiation and distinguishes between symbolism, materialism, and transcendentalism. The transcendentalist, he argues, sees matter as essentially evil, as something that separates man from the freedom and truth he desires. The materialist, as we have seen, regards matter as the sole reality, and admits only the existence of a material world which we perceive with our senses and corroborate by analytic science. The symbolist posits the existence of two worlds, the material and the spiritual, the one manifest and visible, the other hidden and invisible, but the visible material world is seen as the way in which an invisible spiritual essence becomes manifest.

Matter, therefore, may be regarded by the symbolist in two ways, as 'the Divine and physical aspects of the same power.' [16] It is at once the 'garment' of the Divine Imagination and its 'negation', the means by which Christ became incarnate and at the same time the body he had to cast off on the cross. The material manifestation, when regarded as complete in itself, is the means by which a spiritual essence is concealed, but when regarded as a symbol is the means by which a spiritual essence is revealed. The paradox is that a spiritual essence needs a material form to become visible to mortal eyes, but the form which reveals may also conceal. When viewed symbolically, man and the external world become embodiments of a spiritual truth, yet the embodiment is not itself the truth, but only an expression of the truth and is limited by the very form through which the expression is made possible.

A symbol, we may conclude, is the unique way in which a spiritual mood becomes manifest in intellectual or material form. It is at once the visible mortal blossom of an invisible immortal world and a hand 'pointing the way into some divine labyrinth.' [17]

If matter, memory, and sensation, then, are not the sole realities, if they are only the means by which a spiritual essence becomes visible to mortal eyes, it follows that the symbolist looks inwards rather than outwards, to the Christ embodied in his own breast, and not to 'some external will or imagination however divine' in order to discover that spirituality which has become manifest.[18] It follows also that the symbolist recognizes the uniqueness and sacredness of all living forms: he can see infinity in a grain of sand and eternity in an hour. He loves a thing for what it is in itself, not for what it represents, nor for the ulterior purpose to which it can be put. Symbolism, therefore, which is built on the concept of the individual holiness of all living things, concludes in mutual respect and love, but materialism, which emphasizes the consequence of action and the acquisition of possessions, originates in egotism and concludes in law.

III

The symbolist emphasizes rhythm and pattern, the inner elements that distinguish one living form from another, and he condemns all that threatens to destroy uniqueness. Many times throughout his writings Yeats condemns professional theatrical training which distorts the natural rhythms of the human voice and the natural movement of the human body. Rhythm for Yeats is the 'glimmer, the fragrance, the spirit' of all intense life and literature:[19] the symbolic painter loves form and colour, the symbolic poet rhythm and pattern, for through form, colour, sound, and pattern immortal emotion is embodied and evoked. All art, indeed all human actions, have their beginnings in emotion. The purpose of rhythm is to awaken as well as to express emotion, to carry the mind beyond the threshold of waking life, and call into concrete being 'some portion of the divine life, or of the buried reality,'[20] what Yeats calls in *Ideas of Good and Evil* the Great Mind and Great Memory, the dwelling-house of indefinite moods and of permanent images that have become symbols, that is, images which with the artist's death transcend time and place, pass beyond death and become 'living souls' waiting to descend into the hearts of humanity.[21] Man's emotions, those unsolicited impulses behind all action and artistic creation, come to him, Yeats contends, not from the external world or from his individual consciousness, but from this composite mind and buried memory of the universe. The symbolic artist believes that he is the medium of immortal moods, that he receives his spiritual influx from a world beyond. Literature for him becomes 'the expression of moods by the vehicle of symbol',[22] and whether in the passing effects of nature or in permanent effects consciously created by the artist the moods of mankind are constantly being made and remade by bodiless emotions.

Yeats's occult experiments at the time corroborated what he was learning from Blake and Blake's sources, convincing him *first* that 'the borders of our mind are ever shifting, and that many minds can flow into one another, as it were, and create or reveal a single mind, a single energy'; and *second* that 'the borders of our memories are as shifting, and that our memories are a part of one great memory, the memory of Nature herself.'[23] Yeats's occult experiments, in short, convinced him of the existence of a suprasensual emotional world and that this world could be evoked through symbols, whether used consciously, even arbitrarily, in magical experiments, or half consciously by the successor of the magician, the artist.

IV

Symbolism therefore turns from the crude circumstance of the world to the impulse that set action and the world in motion, to emotion in solitude. It concentrates on the essence which beings embody, and in art 'entangles' in complex colours, words, and forms a 'part of the Divine Essence.'[24] It gives voices to dumb things and bodies to bodiless things. It infuses emotional and spiritual significance into all intellectual and material forms, and in turn it sees all material and intellectual forms as expressing an essence which could not be expressed in any other form and as evoking an emotion which could not 'be evoked by any other arrangement of colours and sounds and forms.'[25] The meaning is embodied in the painting, poem, or natural object. With allegory, on the other hand, the literary form that achieved importance with 'the rise of the merchant class in the thirteenth and fourteenth centuries',[26] the meaning can be abstracted from the form, and the painting, poem, or natural object can become an 'irrelevant beauty'.[27] There is little, Yeats contends, that is either spiritual or unique in allegory: things are said that 'could be said as well, or better, in another way':[28]

> A symbol is indeed the only possible expression of some invisible essence, a transparent lamp about a spiritual flame; while allegory is one of the many possible representations of an embodied thing, or familiar principle, and belongs to fancy and not to imagination: the one is a revelation, the other an amusement.[29]

Allegory for Yeats relies on memory and sensation, on reading an abstract meaning into a sensual experience; thus it tends towards an orthodox God and a generalized concept of the world. The symbolist, on the other hand, who sees all things as with the eyes of God and who at the same time believes in many gods, seeks wisdom and emotional significance in particulars, what is 'permanent and characteristic' in all intellectual and material forms:

> "Vision, or imagination," writes Blake, "is a representation of what actually exists, really and unchangeably. Fable, or allegory, is formed by the daughters of Memory." A vision is, that is to

say, a perception of the eternal symbols, about which the world is formed, while allegory is a memory of some natural event into which we read a spiritual meaning. In vision the meaning chooses its own symbol by a kind of affinity, while in the case of allegory we choose out some corporeal accident, and build into our memory of it a little vision, for allegory, according to Blake, contains "some vision" always, and lift it up into a personification of a spiritual or natural meaning.[30]

V

In the beginning of the world, Yeats contends, there was no separation between matter and spirit: when 'a man beheld a natural object the spiritual thing it expressed came at once into his mind.'[31] Woods, waters, hills, valleys, stones — all of the material forms of nature were holy and haunted. A man could apprehend instinctively the spirit which gave a voice to the dumb things that surrounded him. But as the centuries progressed, mind and matter, the inner spiritual meaning and the outer material form, began to separate. Man no longer regarded the external world as an expression of a spiritual essence, but as an entity in itself, having its own laws. He turned from the expression of his own mind to the study of the external world for its own sake:

> man saw and knew the symbol only. The spirit had gone and left the body to itself. This [state] . . . was wholly given over to blind dogma and dead-letter interpretation. A Church not of the law and the prophets but of the law only, it possessed and possesses nothing but ritual and legalities. It is, according to Blake, the state not only of the man of orthodox belief but of the soul which cannot see beyond external nature, for a symbol is to be read in all the worlds and planes of life.[32]

Progress in a materialistic age is thought to come as a consequence of evolution and education, but progress for Yeats was not slow but sudden and miraculous: 'all life is revelation beginning in miracle and enthusiasm, and dying out as it unfolds itself in what we have mistaken for progress.'[33] Materialism, according to Yeats, reaches its high point during the twentieth century, but at this point, when the old order seems on the point of complete triumph, something miraculous happens. Suddenly, inexplicably, the opposite of all that is characteristic of materialistic thought is born. Man, having become enchanted to the outer form, to possessions and the consequences of action, suddenly becomes sated with science, sensation, and analyses of the external world, and he returns instinctively and dramatically to the spiritual world he has neglected for so long:

> We are . . . at a crowning crisis of the world, at the moment when man is about to ascend . . . the stairway he has been descending from the first days. . . . Man has wooed and won the world, and has fallen weary, and not, I think, for a time, but with a weariness that will not end until the last autumn, when the stars shall be blown away like withered leaves.[34]

With the symbolist movement, Yeats believed, this dramatic change, what he later called the Second Coming, was at hand. The art of the old order, he claimed, was the art of the utilitarian, who wrote with regard to the utility of the thing being expressed; the art of the journalist, who wrote to satisfy an ephemeral whim of his public; the art of the rhetorician, who wrote to change the world to his way of thinking. Literature had become scientific, had turned to study and mimesis of the external world, to commentary on the social, humanitarian, and topical interests of the time, to moral judgment and accusation. Literature, in short, had turned into a criticism of visible life rather than a revelation of the invisible world, and it had begun to use as its means of expression the weapons of science, observation, explanation, argument, theory, and erudition.

But Yeats was convinced that literature differed from explanatory and scientific writing 'in being wrought about a mood, or a community of moods, as the body is wrought about an invisible soul;'[35] that the age of criticism would give way to an age of revelation, that belief in a suprasensual world was at hand; that the artist would rid his verse of 'heterogeneous knowledge and irrelevant analysis' and so purify his mind with meditation that he would become 'a vessel of the creative power of God;'[36] that he would disturb the prosperity and peace of the material world, discovering 'immortal moods in mortal desires' and creating 'beings who made the people of this world seem but shadows, and great passions which made our loves and hatreds appear but ephemeral and trivial fantasies'.[37] Literature would become the 'signature or symbol of a mood of the divine imagination'.[38] It would concern itself again with the essence of things rather than with things, with the inner life, the spiritual and the unemphatic. It would open the 'secret doors' of the heart and teach men not the accusation but the 'forgiveness of sins commanded by Christ', awakening in them a sympathy with one another and 'with all living things, sinful and religious alike,'[39] and as men's imaginations became enlarged with sympathy they would put off the limitations of their mortality.

Symbolism, therefore, would alter the substance, style, and form of poetry. Art would be created not for the sake of description of external things or for the presentation of moral opinions, not 'to mirror our own excited faces, or the boughs waving outside the window', but that it might unfold the pictures in the artist's heart. With this change in substance would come a change in style, the substitution of 'wavering, meditative, organic rhythms' for the 'energetic rhythms' that had dominated the poetry of the nineteenth century, the creation of form capable of giving 'a body to something that moves beyond the senses,'[40] an emphasis on words full of subtle, mysterious, complex life, on words and forms behind which glimmered 'a spiritual and passionate mood'.[41]

This sense of symbolic apocalypse dominates Yeats's work during the eighteen-nineties. In 1891 he had linked the coming of the new age to the birth of William Blake:

> In the year 1757 according to the illumination of Emanuel Swedenborg a new age of the world began. The old theological Christian Church from that year out was to be on the wane, and a new dispensation wherein "externals" and "internals," outer observance and interior impulse were one, henceforth crescent in its place. Dogmatic Christianity as I read and as Blake read the "Apocalypse Unveiled" was to give place to the

free religion of ideality and imagination. The old heavens were already, in the spiritual world, rolled away like a scroll and a new heaven and a new earth come to be. In time the new state of things would spread also to the world of men, for revolutions of thought like marriages are made in heaven. The prophesy has been fulfilled. Religious feeling has become a portion of culture instead of a sectarian instinct and the old law of mechanical restraint is giving place in the best minds to the more gentle, if really more exacting rule of refinement and imagination. Blake held himself as set apart by nature and marked out by his birth in the year 1757 as poet of this new rule. "A new heaven is begun, and it is now thirty-three years since its advent" he is to write in 1790 in "The Marriage of Heaven and Hell." [42]

It did not take Yeats long, however, to transfer the new influx of spiritual power to his own time: 'I have always considered myself', he writes at the age of twenty-seven, 'a voice of what I believe to be a greater renaissance — the revolt of the soul against the intellect — now beginning in the world.' [43]

II TWILIGHT AND THE ROSE

The Celtic Twilight, The Secret Rose,
and *Stories of Red Hanrahan*

The Celtic Twilight

The symbolist turns from the barren glass of the outer world to the truth embodied in his own heart. To be brought beyond the limitations of his individual being, however, and into communion with the Great Mind and Memory of the universe, he needs also a 'traditional mythology'.[1] Yeats turned for this tradition and mythology to the legend and lore of his own country, for like Synge and Lady Gregory he believed that the Irish peasant was untouched by the materialism and scientific investigations resulting from the restless Renaissance, that the Irish peasant still maintained contact with the mystery and imagination that existed before man fell a slave to the external world. His search, consequently, was for the traditions which lay buried in peasants' huts and cottages, and his main collection of folk lore and legend, *The Celtic Twilight*, was published in 1893, the same year as the publication of his analysis of the work of William Blake.

The philosophical idea behind 'The Celtic Twilight' has never properly been analysed. Yet when we turn to the first edition of the work, and to other articles Yeats wrote at the time, we find that he himself is explicit as to its meaning:

> There is a moment at twilight in which all men look handsome, all women beautiful; and day by day as he wandered slowly and aimlessly he passed deeper and deeper into that Celtic Twilight, in which heaven and earth so mingle that each seems to have taken upon itself some shadow of the other's beauty. It filled his soul with a desire for he knew not what, it possessed his body with a thirst for unimagined experiences.[2]

There are times, Yeats writes, when the material and spiritual world are 'so near together that it seems as if our earthly chattels were no more than the shadows of things beyond.'[3] Twilight, as we know, is midway between dark and day, one of the 'stitches' joining the natural and spiritual worlds,[4] a world where men seem as remote from mortal life as the immortal images of art. In his work on Blake, Yeats had associated the material world with winter and darkness and the spiritual world with light and full consciousness. The Celtic twilight, the world of the folk, was midway between the two, a 'covenant' between spiritual beauty and the 'beauty of the world.'[5] In the half-light, then, heaven and earth commingled; spiritual essences still filled material forms, and the forms themselves seemed but the shadows of some greater reality beyond.

To the peasant, Yeats writes, 'everything is a symbol':[6] he can perceive the correspondence between sensuous form and supersensuous meaning and can recognize instinctively the spirit which gives a voice to the dumb things that surround him. Not distinguishing clearly between natural and supernatural, and believing instinctively that all nature is full of invisible spirits that can be perceived by those willing to look beyond the veil of the senses, the peasant sees everything as enchanted: hills, valleys, woods, waters, monumental stones. He is filled with a sense of the sanctity, mystery, and threat of everything that surrounds him. The legendary associations of topographical sites are fresh in his mind. To the peasant the land is still a haunted holy land.

Man's ability to perceive the spiritual essences embodied in material forms slowly perishes through the centuries. Machines and cities kill the 'passive meditative mind'; education enlarges the egotistic 'self-moving mind,'[7] making the soul less sensitive to spiritual influences. As life becomes more ordered and deliberate, Yeats argues, the 'supernatural world sinks farther away';[8] everything is confined, weighed, measured; even art becomes the property of the privileged few. The body, once a 'beautiful woven web,' becomes imperfect and incomplete, 'like a bundle of cords knotted together and flung into a corner.'[9]

But in places where the traditional order of life remains unbroken, in folk life where people still linger 'on the edges of vision'[10] and learn to live with spirits that haunt their solitary world, everything is 'unbounded and immortal': the passions, hatred and love, are not measured, and 'seek no mortal thing but their own infinity'.[11] The Celtic peasant, therefore, does not live in a shrunken over-defined world. Nor does he concern himself with probability or necessity, but only with the expression of emotion. He has within him 'the vast and vague extravagance that lies at the bottom of the Celtic heart',[12] and so ample is his imagination and so deep his belief in legend and lore that he can sometimes see with mortal eyes legendary figures, ghosts, goblins, fairies, purgatory, heaven and hell. In his rambling moralless tales, full of wonder and emotion because created by the community at large, he 'mounts to the infinite by the ladder of the impossible.'[13] The tales become not a criticism of life but an exaggerated expression of life.

In folk life, Yeats argues, instinct does the work of reason. Men have the leisure for the luxury of meditation. The best tales and thoughts are gathered and refined over the centuries and pass on unchanged from generation to generation. The folk thus possess a permanent living tradition, images and emotions which carry 'their memories backward thousands of years.'[14] They can commune with the dead generations, and receive from the Great Mind and Memory images that come to visionary and meditative minds:

> Images form themselves in our minds perpetually as if they were reflected in some pool. . . . We can make our minds so like still water that beings gather about us that they may see, it may be, their own images, and so live for a moment with a clearer, perhaps even a fiercer life because of our quiet.[15]

The language of the folk, also, is refined throughout the centuries, but yet has not become habitual; it retains its emotional expressiveness, its animation of rhythm and idiom; words and verses are capable of embodying and suggesting a mystery beyond what is materially apparent.

Tradition, religion, and the deprivations of material life had made the folk painfully aware of the distance which separated the dream they craved in their hearts from the imperfections of mortal life. Through their tales, their compensating dreams, they sought to escape daily circumstance, to reshape the material world according to the spiritual vision in their hearts, and call into concrete being what modern materialistic men would call the 'unreal' world. Modern men, believing that material life is complete and can be happy, delight, Yeats suggests, in 'tales that end in marriage bells',[16] but folk people, fully cognizant of the inherent tragedy and imperfections of unaccommodated man, are attracted to tales that end in death and parting; death to the folk is not the end but the beginning of wisdom and power:

> Life was so weighed down by the emptiness of the great forests and by the mystery of all things, and by the greatness of its own desires, and, as I think, by the loneliness of much beauty; and seemed so little and so fragile and so brief, that nothing could be more sweet in the memory than a tale that ended in death and parting, and than a wild and beautiful lamentation. Men . . . mourn[ed] . . . because they had been born and must die with their great thirst unslaked.[17]

Yeats, then, was attracted by the sense of the brevity of life and the acceptance of the conditions of life in folk literature. Folk people had the propensity for meditation and vision; they were isolated from the material world, were uninfluenced by science or fashion, were not motivated by ulterior purpose or popularity, and had more sympathy with their fellows than with the law which constrained and punished them. Like the symbolic poet, peasant visionaries sought to capture in imaginative idiom and tale 'some high, impalpable mood', to express 'a something that lies beyond the range of expression',[18] to create in the deprivation of material life a mask or compensating dream. They maintained a passionate interest in human life and at the same time held that the material world was but a shadow of some greater reality. The land about them was a haunted and holy land. Like great artists, these visionaries had the power to mythologize places and people, to transform mortal men and women into immortal images, to transform, for example, Mary Hynes and Raftery into 'perfect symbols of the sorrow of beauty and of the magnificence and penury of dreams.'[19] And like great artists, peasant visionaries possessed a living permanent tradition, traditional images and stories passed on unchanged from generation to generation.

It was to the folk myths and literature of his own country that Yeats turned to find his 'traditional mythology'. The symbolic poet, he maintained, must learn what the common people knew instinctively, sanctity of place and a sense of tradition. His themes must be taken not from circumscribed history but from the mythological tales of the people, and his work must have the daring and imaginative impulse that motives all folk literature: there are moods, Yeats writes, 'which shall find no expression unless there be men who dare to mix heaven, hell, purgatory, and fairyland together, or even to set the heads of beasts to the bodies of men, or to thrust the souls of men into the heart of rocks'.[20]

Folk life is therefore 'the soil where all great art is rooted.'[21] Indeed, Yeats could see no essential difference between folk poetry and poetry with a sophisticated literary lineage. The one presupposed knowledge of the unwritten tradition, the other knowledge of the written tradition. The one used the 'unchanging speech of the poets',[22] the other the vivid living language of the people. Both had tradition and 'ancestry', and both suggested a mystery beyond what was actually embodied in the verses:

> All the greatest literature of the world has been of one or other of two kinds, it has been either altogether aristocratic or altogether of the people. I mean by aristocratic that it has been shaped by men like Dante and like Homer and like Shakespeare, by great artists who have had to guide their hands a long descended learned tradition of the arts perfected by master after master, in deliberate leisure and in careful detachment from the world. The literature that is of the people on the other hand, and it is on this literature the literature of the aristocracy [is based], is a literature of stories and little folk songs imagined by no one can tell who, and handed on from generation to generation by peasant story-tellers and by peasant singers. The literature that has arisen between these two, the arts that have no antiquity and no high breeding, are either of an inferior kind however excellent of their kind, or they are merely popular, merely of the moment and will pass away.[23]

Poetry which had passed as popular poetry, Yeats posits in his essay on 'Poetry and Tradition', was not from the people at all, but from the materialistic middle classes who had 'unlearned' the unwritten tradition and had not learned the written one: it is a poetry with 'manifest logic' and rhetoric, without 'breeding and ancestry', and is popular because it is easily understood.

Yeats's great aim was to bridge the written and unwritten traditions, to establish a learned literary tradition on emotions that came from the heart of the people, and so create from the shock of new material and from a tradition that had never found expression in sophisticated literature a new style, a new mood of the soul.

The Secret Rose

Through his collections of folk lore and legends, then, stories of 'half-forgotten innocent old places',[24] Yeats sought to re-awaken 'imaginative tradition', to carry the mind back to 'forgotten mythologies', for these stories, he claimed, ascend 'like medieval genealogies through unbroken dignities to the beginning of the world.'[25] His own stories which he wrote during the eighteen-nineties, the strange stories that form the substance of *The Secret Rose*, although written at different times and in different styles, and without any definite plan, have, as Yeats indicated in his Dedication to the first edition, 'but one subject, the war of spiritual with natural order.'

In 'The Binding of the Hair', omitted from the revised editions of *The Secret Rose*, the spiritual is represented by the bard Aodh, by the beauty he serves, and the moods he is capable of creating. In one moment he can stir the massive hosts with heroic courage and impatience for battle, and in the next he can stir in the heart of a queen the subtlest of emotions:

> the young queen sat among her women, straight and still like a white candle, and listened as though there was no tale in the world but this tale of Aodh's, for the enchantment of his dream-heavy voice was in her ears; the enchantment of his dream-distraught history in her mind: how he would live now in the raths of kings, now alone in the great forest; how, despite the grey hairs mingling before their time with the dark of his beard, he was blown hither and thither by love and anger; how, according to his mood, he would fly now from one man and with blanched face, and would now show an extreme courage one man against many; and, above all, how he had sat continually by her great chair telling of forays and battles, to hearten her war-weary men-at-arms, or chaunting histories and songs laden with gentler destinies for her ears alone, or, more often still, listening in silence to the rustling of her dress.
>
> He sang now of anger and not of love, for it was needful to fill the hearts of her men-at-arms with thirst of battle that her days might have peace; yet over all the tale hovered a mournful beauty not of battle, and from time to time he would compare the gleam of a sword to the brightness of her eyes; or the dawn breaking on a morning of victory to the glimmering of her breast. As the tale, and its songs, which were like the foam upon a wave, flowed on, it wrapped the men-at-arms as in a tide of fire, and its vehement passages made them clash their swords

upon their shields and shout an always more clamorous approval. At last it died out in a chaunt of triumph over battle-cars full of saffron robes and ornaments of gold and silver, and over troops of young men and young girls with chains of bronze about their ankles; and the men shouted and clashed their swords upon their shields for a long time. The queen sat motionless for a little, and then leaned back in her chair so that its carved back made one dark tress fall over her cheek. Sighing a long, inexplicable sigh, she bound the tress about her head and fastened it with a golden pin. Aodh gazed at her, the fierce light fading in his eyes, and began to murmur something over to himself, and presently, taking the five-stringed cruit from the ground, half knelt before her, and softly touched the strings. The shouters fell silent, for they saw that he would praise the queen, as his way was when the tales were at an end; and in the silence he struck three notes, as soft and sad as though they were the cooing of doves over the Gates of Death.[26]

Both armies are destroyed in the battle, and their bodies left on the desolate plains to be devoured by birds of prey. The bard has also fallen, but his severed head chants to the queen who treads among the strewn dead bodies the delicate poem which has immortalized one mortal gesture:

Of a sudden, a sweet, tremulous song came from a bush near them. They hurried towards the spot, and saw a head hanging from the bush by its dark hair; and the head was singing, and this was the song it sung:

> Fasten your hair with a golden pin,
>   And bind up every wandering tress;
>   I bade my heart build these poor rhymes:
> It worked at them, day out, day in,
>   Building a sorrowful loveliness
>   Out of the battles of old times.
>
> You need but lift a pearl-pale hand,
>   And bind up your long hair and sigh;

> And all men's hearts must burn and beat;
> And candle-like foam on the dim sand,
> And stars climbing the dew-dropping sky,
> Live but to light your passing feet.[27]

The massive armies prove powerless over matter, and must suffer the fate of all who serve material things; but the bard, by his mastery over mood and spirit, achieves immortality both for himself and for the beauty he has seen manifested.

Mere material death cannot destroy the mood a poet articulates, nor can it destroy the passion expressed between a man and a woman. When Costello dances with his true love Una in 'Proud Costello' there falls over the lovers a 'weariness with the world, the melancholy, the pity one for the other, which is the exultation of love.'[28] Unlike Hanrahan, Costello sees in his beloved the embodiment of all the spiritual and physical beauty that has been manifested in the world, but the lovers are prevented from union by their feuding families, a materialistic piper, and their own pride. It is only when Costello, with his indifference to material possession, recklessly gives up his body that they achieve union, and the ash-trees over their graves weave 'their branches together' and mingle 'their leaves.'[29]

'The Rose of Shadow', omitted like 'The Binding of the Hair' from the revised editions of *The Secret Rose*, is more violent, for it is not the love of innocent young man for innocent young woman that is depicted, but the love of a brutal violent man for a young innocent girl whom he seduces 'through that love of strength which is deep in the heart of even the subtlest among them.'[30] Although he is killed in vengeance by the girl's brother, he returns on the anniversary of his death, dramatically, violently, to shatter the complacent world of the girl's family and to claim his captive waiting love.

The strange shock of these stories is carefully calculated and carefully enhanced by the violence of the characters who represent the spiritual order. In 'The Crucifixion of the Outcast', for example, by a savage reversal, the spiritual order is represented by the outcast, the bard, and the natural order by a community of monks. The monks are dedicated to material order and peace, and the bard who disturbs their prosperity and peace is crucified. But while the reader can easily perceive the hypocrisy and self-interestedness of the Abbot's condemnation of the bard in the 1897 version of the tale ('Brother, the bards and gleemen are an evil race, ever cursing and ever stirring up the people, and immoral and immoderate in all things, and heathen in their hearts'),[31] to the unwary reader of the revised edition the crucifixion may appear to be justified: 'Brother, there is not one of these bards and gleemen who has not scattered his bastards through the five kingdoms, and if they slit a purse or a throat, and it is always one or the other, it never comes into their heads to confess and do penance.'[32] To the bard, however, the monks are the 'haters of life and joy', the race which 'melts the bones of the people with cowardice and with deceit'.[33]

Yeats based his tale on the eleventh-century romance, *The Vision of MacConglinne*, edited by Kuno Meyer in 1892.[34] In the original, however, the bard eludes the crucifixion and gains the king's favour, but in Yeats's version of the tale the Abbot consciously and successfully baits the trap for the bard's destruction. But although the bard is preyed upon by monks, beggars, beasts, and birds, his body and the material world mean little to him. He is sustained to the end by the vision of the ideal world he holds in his heart, and it is this vision which lingers in our minds:

> I have travelled the bare road, and by the edges of the sea; and the tattered doublet of parti-coloured cloth upon my back and the torn pointed shoes upon my feet have ever irked me, because of the towered city full of noble raiment which was in my heart. And I have been the more alone upon the roads and by the sea because I heard in my heart the rustling of the rose-bordered dress of her who is more subtle than Aengus the Subtle-hearted, and more full of the beauty of laughter than Conan the Bald, and more full of the wisdom of tears than White-breasted Deirdre, and more lovely than a bursting dawn to them that are lost in the darkness.[35]

It is interesting, in the light of Yeats's later work, that the ideal world is conceived not only in terms of the Rose but also in terms of a 'towered city full of noble raiment'.

The pattern of *The Secret Rose* is not simple. It is not merely a matter of bard against monk, of pagan against Christian, of energy against repression. Where Yeats had emphasized the fierce oppression of the monks in 'The Crucifixion of the Outcast,' he emphasizes their piety in 'The Curse of the Fires and the Shadows' and their capacity for ecstasy in 'Where There is Nothing, there is God'. The dedicated Knight in 'Out of the Rose' defends the prayerful old man and destroys the sacrilegious plunderers, while the old man in 'The Old Men of the Twilight', although detached from the world and dedicated to his rosary, preserves his passion for possession and plunder, and is consequently denied the contact with the supernatural which is offered him. In 'The Curse of the Fires and the Shadows' the supernatural intervenes to destroy those who plunder for mere material reward: 'Woe unto all who have struck down those who have lived in the Light of the Lord,' the dying abbot proclaims, 'for they shall wander among shadows and among fires!'[36]

The Secret Rose offers no certain way by which spiritual fulfilment can be achieved: no 'human soul is like any other human soul, and therefore the love of God for any human soul is infinite, for no other soul can satisfy the same need in God.'[37] Some of the characters in *The Secret Rose* find fulfilment by uncompromising expression of the spiritual energy hidden in their hearts, while others find it by dedication and austerity. 'Where There is Nothing, there is God', which is built around a cabalistic concept, shows how those who turn from the material world, who go 'to live in the wild places and among the wild beasts',[38] can receive wisdom and knowledge directly from God: God is where there is nothing, where the material world has been consumed within the mind. 'The Heart of the Spring' depicts the culmination of an old man's search for the spiritual:

> I have fasted and laboured when others would sink into the sleep of old age. . . . I have sought through all my life to find the secret of life. I was not happy in my youth, for I knew that it would pass; and I was not happy in my manhood, for I knew that age was coming; and so I gave myself, in youth and manhood and age, to the search for the Great Secret. I longed for a life whose abundance would fill centuries, I scorned the life of

fourscore winters. I would be — no, I *will* be!—like the ancient gods of the land.[39]

Through lonely labour, study, and magical experiments he is led by his thirst for the perfect to the spirit which inhabits all material forms, 'the beings who dwell in the waters and among the hazels and oak-trees,' the ancient gods who 'watch over the loveliness of the earth.'[40] Those who seek easy completion in material life, like the old man's boy-servant, find initial fulfilment with wives and children, but they are defeated by death; the old man, on the other hand, enters in the end into the 'eternal kingdom' of his youth, the 'heart of the spring', and his soul is reborn as a bird.

'God has made out of His abundance a separate wisdom for everything which lives,'[41] concludes the old man in 'The Heart of the Spring'. All of the characters who achieve spiritual triumph in *The Secret Rose* follow, in different ways, the light and longing of their own hearts, and having seen the truth turn from the 'corrupted' material world. Perhaps the clearest exposition of this theme, the central theme of the volume, is made by the Knight in 'Out of the Rose':

> I was one of those in the Order who always longed for more arduous labours in the service of the truth that can only be understood within the heart. At last there came to us a Knight of Palestine, to whom the truth of truths had been revealed by God Himself. He had seen a great Rose of Fire, and a Voice out of the Rose had told him how men would turn from the light of their own hearts, and bow down before outer order and outer fixity, and that then the light would cease, and none escape the curse except the foolish good man who could not think, and the passionate wicked man who would not. Already, the Voice told him, the light of the heart was shining with less lustre, and as it paled, an infection was touching the world with corruption; and none of those who had seen clearly the truth could enter into the Kingdom of God, which is in the Heart of the Rose, if they stayed on willingly in the corrupted world; and so they must prove their anger against the Powers of Corruption by dying in the service of the Rose. . . . At first we thought to die

more readily by fasting to death in honour of some saint; but this he told us was evil, for we did it for the sake of death, and thus took out of the hands of God the choice of the time and manner of our death, and by so doing made His power the less. We must choose our service for its excellence, and for this alone, and leave it to God to reward us at His own time and in His own manner.[42]

Early in the eighteen-nineties Yeats had emphasized the spiritual essence embodied in material forms, but in some of the stories of *The Secret Rose* the spiritual and natural worlds are beginning to drift apart. 'The Wisdom of the King' provides an example of Yeats's ambivalence towards the supernatural world, an attitude which he explores in *Stories of Red Hanrahan*, *Rosa Alchemica*, *The Tables of the Law*, and *The Adoration of the Magi*. The story hints at the impossibility of fulfilment through natural pursuits, once men's eyes have been opened to supernatural wisdom, once the heart has been emptied of its mortal dream:

> While they listened to him his words seemed to make all darkness light and filled their hearts like music. . . . A number indeed did live differently afterwards, but their new life was less excellent than the old: some among them had long served a good cause, but when they heard him praise it, they returned to their own lands to find what they had loved less lovable, for he had taught them how little divides the false and true; others, again, who had served no cause, but had sought in peace the welfare of their own households, found their bones softer and less ready for toil, for he had shown them greater purposes; and numbers of the young, when they had heard him upon all these things, remembered certain strange words that made ordinary joys nothing, and sought impossible joys and grew unhappy.[43]

The wisdom of the king is in recognizing that supernatural wisdom and natural law are incompatible:

> Men of law, why did you make me sin against the laws? Men of verse, why did you make me sin against the secrecy of wisdom? — for law was made by man for the welfare of man,

but wisdom the gods have made, and no man shall live by its light, for it and the hail and the rain and the thunder follow a way that is deadly to mortal things.[44]

The King, in unwittingly adapting supernatural wisdom to natural laws, has sinned against both. For what passes as natural wisdom is born from man's will; what is given as supernatural wisdom is born in a mood.

Stories of Red Hanrahan

The theme we have been tracing in 'The Wisdom of the King', the separation of spiritual and material, is the theme which permeates the *Stories of Red Hanrahan*, collected first in *The Secret Rose*, and later rewritten with Lady Gregory's help during 1903 - 4.[45]

The changes in the first story are significant. In *The Secret Rose* version Hanrahan purchases the 'Book of the Great Dhoul' to convey to his neighbours the impression that he has dealings with the Devil, and so revenge himself on them for suggesting that he received his poetic inspiration from the Sidhe. After he has succeeded in this purpose, however, he hungers to read the Book of which hitherto he had been 'mortally afraid'. He discovers a formula for invoking spirits, and always having longed to gaze upon the Sidhe, he follows the formula, and Cleena, the Queen of the Munster fairies, appears before him. In this version of the story Hanrahan is clearly the active protagonist, much as Yeats himself is the active protagonist when he invokes ideal beauty in 'To the Rose upon the Rood of Time'. In the revised version of the story, however, Hanrahan has become the passive protagonist, in the same way as Yeats has become the passive protagonist in 'The Hosting of the Sidhe': Hanrahan is enchanted by an old man with a pack of cards, who changes one of the cards into a hare and the rest into a pack of hounds which Hanrahan follows. He is led to a great house and to a woman seated in a high chair, 'the most beautiful woman the world ever saw, having a long pale face and flowers about it, but she had the tired look of one that had been long waiting.'[46] It is the Queen of the immortal Sidhe. Hanrahan is too over-awed to speak 'to so beautiful a woman, and in so grand a place', whereupon the four grey old women who attend the Queen accuse him:

one of them said, "He has no wish for us"; and another said, "He is weak, he is weak"; and another said, "He is afraid"; and the last said, "His wits are gone from him." And then they all said, "Echtge, daughter of the Silver Hand, must stay in her sleep. It is a pity, it is a great pity."

And then the woman that was like a queen gave a very sad sigh. . . ."[47]

The vision passes and Hanrahan is doomed to wander unfulfilled in the world, consumed with his vision of the immortal Sidhe:

"It is a pity for him that refuses the call of the daughters of the Sidhe, for he will find no comfort in the love of the women of the earth to the end of life and time, and the cold of the grave is in his heart for ever. It is death he has chosen; let him die, let him die, let him die." [48]

In the *Secret Rose* version of the story, however, the Queen of the Sidhe, Cleena, is invoked and appears in Hanrahan's cabin, first in immortal form, and later in mortal form: 'you have sought for me everywhere and in everything, though without knowing what you sought, and now I have come to you and taken on mortality that I may share your sorrow.' [49] Hanrahan's memory of mortal women, however, and of the trouble they had caused him, can only lead him to denounce and reject Cleena: 'Woman, begone out of this. I have had enough of women. I am weary of women. I am weary of life. . . . It was not you I loved, but the woman of the Shee.' [50] Cleena in retaliation places a curse upon Hanrahan:

"Owen Hanrahan the Red, you have looked so often upon the dust that when the Rose has blossomed there you think it but a pinch of coloured dust; but now I lay upon you a curse, and you shall see the Rose everywhere, in the noggin, in woman's eye, in drifting phantoms, and seek to come to it in vain; it shall waken a fire in your heart, and in your feet, and in your hands. A sorrow of all sorrows is upon you, Owen Hanrahan the Red." [51]

Hanrahan, therefore, separates the spiritual and material worlds. He is able to enchant many mortal women, but he sees in them only the 'deciduous blossom of the dust and not the eternal beauty.'[52] He is unable to see in his mortal beloved the embodiment of immortal beauty. When the spiritual is miraculously offered to him in mortal form his memories of mortality prevent him from accepting it. He is cursed consequently to see the spiritual in immaterial phantoms, to seek it in vain. He can serve his unattainable ideal in his verse, as in 'Red Hanrahan's Song about Ireland', but he can never be fulfilled in mortal life and must go to his grave with the great dichotomy unresolved, the dichotomy between the spirituality he craves in his heart and the body he is afflicted with in mortal life.

He retains his power to enchant mortal women, as in 'The Twisting of the Rope':

> We will wander on and on, you and I. Do you not hear the song of the great white roads, calling, calling? We will listen to the cuckoo, we will see the salmon leap in the rivers, we will sleep under the green oak leaves. . . . Death will never find us in the heart of the wood. . . . And even if death find us, how will it matter? Even if the rains beat upon us, how will it matter? Even if the winds blow upon us, how will it matter? We shall have found that for which the woods spread their tents of green, and the stars light their candles.[53]

In 'The Twisting of the Rope', however, he loses the young girl by a ruse of her over-protective mother, but even when he succeeds in winning mortal women he quickly tires of them.

Hanrahan's inability to bridge the spiritual and mortal world results in a greater awareness of his own mortality, a cleavage between dream and reality. Witness for example:

> Grey forms, half seen, half felt, seemed to gather about him and to walk upon the sea. And among them Cleena of the wave passed by, *no longer marred by a human body*, but laughing and mocking under a crown of rubies.[54]

And:

> immense shadows seemed to be taking him to themselves, disembodying him away into the dim life of the Powers that have

never lived in mortal bodies. All night they passed through his dreams crowned with rubies, and having roses in their hands; and in the morning he awoke, a rough-clad peasant, shivering on the earthern floor.[55]

The dichotomy between spiritual longing and material decay, and the impossibility of ever reconciling the two, increases as the stories continue, and Hanrahan's progressive deterioration towards death is depicted in terms of his relations with women: in the first story he communes with an immortal queen; in the second with an impressionable girl; in the third with a middle-aged woman who is weary of selling herrings; in the fourth the sight of a young girl impresses on him a sense of his own old age; in the fifth he has a terrible vision of a procession of lovers, and in this procession he reads his own fate. First he sees a long line of beautiful young men and women whose faces are 'full of a proud tenderness, and pale as with a quenchless desire of august and mournful things'; then lovers who have 'heart-shaped mirrors instead of hearts', lovers 'looking on their own faces in one another's mirrors'; then women pursued by men, their heads 'beyond all beauty', their bodies 'shadows without life'; and finally a pair of dark 'half-hidden forms', Diarmuid and Dervorgilla, who interpret the vision:

> Those that passed the first . . . are the famous lovers of old time, Blanid and Deirdre, and Grania, and their dear friends, and a multitude less known, but not less beloved; and because they sought in one another no blossom of mere youth, but a beauty coeval with the night and with the stars, the night and the stars hold them for ever from the unpeaceful and the perishing, despite the battle and the bitterness their love wrought in the world. Those who came next, O man, who still breathe the sweet air, and have the mirrors in their hearts, are sung by no bards, because they sought only to triumph one over the other, and so to prove their strength and beauty, and fashioned out of this a kind of love. The women with shadowy bodies desired neither to triumph nor to love, but only to be loved, and there is no blood in their hearts or in their bodies until it flow through them from a kiss, and their life is but for a moment.[56]

Diarmuid and Dervorgilla, like Hanrahan, have loved 'only the blossom of manhood and of womanhood in one another,' and their fate is that the lover beholds the beloved as 'a dead body dropping in decay'.

In the sixth and final story everything is infected with decay:

> The old yew above his cabin looked the more malignant from dwelling at so great a height an outcast from among its kind, and seemed to uplift its dark branches like withered hands threatening the stars, and the blue deep they swim in, with the coming of decay and shadowy old age.[57]

At the moment of his death Hanrahan accepts something he has been unwilling to accept throughout his life, that frail mortality can embody immortal beauty:

> He saw the withered earthern face and withered earthern arms, and for all his weakness shrank further towards the wall; and then faint white arms, wrought as of glistening cloud, came out of the mud-stiffened tatters and were clasped about his body; and a voice that sounded faint and far, but was of a marvellous distinctness, whispered in his ears: "you will seek me no longer upon the breasts of women." [58]

The curse of Hanrahan is that he cannot die, like the May blossoms, in the time of beauty, but that he must suffer the indignities of old age. But the 'mighty memories' of the beauty he has lost and which presumably he will find again in the grave Yeats needs in his own old age:

> Did all old men and women, rich and poor,
> Who trod upon these rocks or passed this door,
> Whether in public or in secret rage
> As I do now against old age?
> But I have found an answer in those eyes
> That are impatient to be gone;
> Go therefore; but leave Hanrahan,
> For I need all his mighty memories.[59]

III FROM DREAM TO VISION:

Rosa Alchemica, The Tables of the Law,
and *The Adoration of the Magi*

I

Rosa Alchemica, The Tables of the Law, and *The Adoration of the Magi* present in uncompromising terms the apocalyptic annunciation of a new dispensation. The structure of these stories is also similar: each has as narrator an orthodox Christian; through this technique Yeats was not only able to explore his own ambivalence towards the new annunciation, but he was also able to provide a dramatic balance between the orthodoxy of his readers and the strangeness of the message he had to impart.

The situation in *Rosa Alchemica* is complicated by the fact that the narrator holds certain convictions that Yeats himself may have held at one point during the eighteen-nineties. The narrator has driven everything from him except dreams; he has separated himself completely from the external world and surrounded himself with paintings, tapestries, sculptures and literature. Through art and meditation he believes that he can experience the range of human passion without its bitterness:

> I had gathered about me all gods because I believed in none, and experienced every pleasure because I gave myself to none, but held myself apart, individual, indissoluble, a mirror of polished steel.[1]

The narrator is an alchemist, or more precisely a writer on alchemy, having just completed a 'little work' called *Rosa Alchemica*. Early in his researches he had discovered that the alchemical doctrine 'was no merely chemical fantasy,' but a philosophy applied 'to the world, to the elements and to man himself': alchemists sought not merely to fashion gold out of common metals, but they regarded this 'as part of a universal transmutation of all things into some divine and imperishable substance'. Consequently, the narrator's work, *Rosa*

Alchemica, becomes 'a fanciful reverie over the transmutation of life into art, and a cry of measureless desire for a world made wholly of essences.'[2]

But the narrator is not content. He is, he believes, living among 'immortal essences,' yet he experiences no 'miraculous ecstasy.' The art with which he has surrounded himself belongs to a divine world of which he has no part. His mortality mocks his thirst for spiritual perfection. With the realization that the ultimate alchemical act, the 'transmutation of the weary heart into a weariless spirit,' is as far from him as ever, he desires the destruction and dissolution of all mortal things: 'all must be dissolved before the divine substance, material gold or immaterial ecstasy, awake.'[3]

The paradox that the narrator himself does not seem to realize is that while he calls for the dissolution of mortal things he has to this point held himself 'indissoluble, a mirror of polished steel.' On the one hand he attempts to shut out the external world, but on the other hand he wishes to experience all human activity vicariously through the art he has collected. He is too a *collector* of art, of 'gold born in the crucibles of others',[4] rather than an artist himself. What he does not realize is that it is only through the constant activity of art, not in merely surrounding oneself with works of art, that ecstasy can be experienced and a changing heart transmuted for a moment into a changeless work of art. But this transmutation is not a single definitive alchemical act: as long as mortal breath remains the artist must return to the material world to which, during the moment of creative activity, he has become indifferent. Life, therefore, when lived intensely, becomes an endless oscillation between spiritual vision and material life, and death becomes the consummation of the ecstatic process, for at death the weary human artist can become the weariless spiritual thing he has created: the poet can become the poem; the dancer can become the dance.

To the narrator of *Rosa Alchemica,* art, although divine, is a dead reality. He does not realize that ecstasy for a human being is eternal but momentary, that the ultimate alchemical act is a dream and can never be completed as long as mortal breath remains. Rather than seeing man and nature as merely the mirror of reality, the expression of a divine mood embodied in the human breast, the narrator, although an alchemist, believes that the mirror is the reality. He is in a way like the materialist Yeats describes in his writings on Blake in that he works from effect to cause and does not see things as with the eyes of angels, does not realize that physical effects, like artistic creations, are only the way in which a spiritual essence becomes visible. The narrator in short is not a true symbolist. Like Hanrahan, he is poised uncomfortably between the material and spiritual, the definite and indefinite worlds.

The narrator has been caught in an alchemical dream. With the invitation of Michael Robartes to join the Order of the Alchemical Rose, however, he is provided with an opportunity to be taken from the ineffectuality of dream to the ecstasy of vision.

Dream is the vain attempt to transmute the material world into a divine world: total ecstasy is impossible because complete transmutation is impossible. Vision, on the other hand, brings beautiful coherence, a sense of 'illumination and exaltation',[5] as men, eyes blank to the material world, receive inspiration directly from the spiritual world, the disembodied soul of the universe. The narrator's error has been in attempting to gather the gods about him, instead of throwing himself at their feet. For man, Michael Robartes asserts, can only do one of two things: forget that he is miserable and lose himself in the activity of the material world *or* 'seek a mystical union with the multitude who govern this world and time.'[6] Man is not 'indissoluble' but merely the medium through which an immortal mood can be expressed: in 'this way all great events were accomplished; a mood, a divinity, or a demon, first descending like a faint sigh into men's minds and then changing their thoughts and their actions'.[7] The new symbolic religion which was about to sweep the world was itself born in a mood:

> I remembered, as I read, that mood which Edgar Poe found in a wine-cup, and how it passed into France and took possession of Baudelaire, and from Baudelaire passed to England and the Pre-Raphaelites, and then again returned to France, and still wanders the world, enlarging its power as it goes, awaiting the time when it shall be, perhaps, alone, or, with other moods, master over a great new religion, and an awakener of the fanatical wars

that hovered in the gray surges, and forget the wine-cup where it was born.[8]

To this point the narrator has believed that man is complete in so far as 'he can make his mind reflect everything with indifferent precision like a mirror,' but the mirror is only a dead reflector and, as a visionary voice asserts, 'is broken into numberless pieces'.[9] Man must turn from the mirror of nature to the source of energy and vision. Man is a shadow, not an existence complete in himself, and artistic creations which men believe but shadows are in reality the eternal gods:

> "countless divinities . . . have taken upon themselves spiritual bodies in the minds of modern poets and romance-writers. . . . The many think humanity made these divinities, and that it can unmake them again; but we who have seen them pass in rattling harness, and in soft robes, and heard them speak with articulate voices while we lay in death-like trance, know that they are always making and unmaking humanity, which is indeed but the trembling of their lips. . . . They have come to us; they have come to us," the voice began again; "all that have ever been in your reverie, all that you have met with in books. There is Lear, his head still wet with the thunder-storm, and he laughs because you thought yourself an existence who are but a shadow, and him a shadow who is an eternal God; and there is Beatrice, with her lips half parted in a smile, as though all the stars were about to pass away in a sigh of love; and there is the mother of the God of humility . . . but she holds in her hand the rose whose every petal is a god; and there, O, swiftly she comes! is Aphrodite under a twilight falling from the wings of numberless sparrows, and about her feet are the grey and white doves." [10]

The more gods men commune with, Michael Robartes announces, the more they grow in imagination and understanding. Devotion to one God produces a 'limited sense of beauty,'[11] and when men serve a God of humility and sorrow, as they have been doing for almost two thousand years, they renounce their own divinity and turn 'from the unfolding of their separate hearts'.[12]

The new age, Michael Robartes announces in *Rosa Alchemica*, will be born from the corruption of a declining Christianity, and, what is interesting in the light of what Yeats wrote later in *A Vision*, 'plunge the world into a night as obscure as that which followed the downfall of the classical world.'[13] Men would reject a God of humility and sorrow, would commune with many gods, and turn from the definite world to the 'teeming, fantastic inner life' of the soul. Ineffectual dream would be replaced by ecstatic vision, and men, realizing the independent reality of emotion and thought, would give themselves to immortal moods which would in turn shape spiritual bodies out of the substance of their hearts.

With the imminent possibility of the violent disruption of the social and spiritual order, the destruction of everything he has known and cultivated, and at the prospect of being carried off into some indefinite and passionate world, the narrator is filled with terror. Under Michael Robartes's 'mesmeric'[14] influence he senses the dissolution of all his fixed principles and habits and the birth of desires and ambitions which are alien to his 'orderly and careful' life:

> I was being lifted out of the tide of flame, and felt my memories, my hopes, my thoughts, my will, everything I held to be myself, melting away; then I seemed to rise through numberless companies of beings who were, I understood, in some way more certain than thought, each wrapped in his eternal moment, in the perfect lifting of an arm, in a little circlet of rhythmical words, in dreaming with dim eyes and half-closed eyelids. . . . All things that had ever lived seemed to come and dwell in my heart, and I in theirs; and I had never again known mortality or tears, had I not suddenly fallen from the certainty of vision into the uncertainty of dream, and become a drop of molten gold falling with immense rapidity, through a night elaborate with stars, and all about me a melancholy exultant wailing.[15]

The vision leaves him powerless to do other than accompany Michael Robartes to the Temple of the Alchemical Rose, and at the sight of the Temple he is filled with fascination and fear: 'One part of my mind mocked this fantastic terror, but the other, the part that still lay half plunged in vision, listened to the clash of unknown armies, and shuddered at unimaginable fanaticisms, that hung in those grey leaping waves.'[16] He is half-initiated into the Order by an ancient dance, for rhythm rather than alchemy is 'the wheel of Eternity, on which alone the transient and accidental could be broken, and the spirit set free.'[17]

Some time after the elaborate ceremony, the narrator, like Hanrahan, awakens, and the 'immense rose wrought in mosaic' which had covered the ceiling of the Temple is now seen as a 'roughly painted rose'; the walls, too, which during the ceremony had seemed to be filled with mosaics 'glimmering like rubies and sapphires' are now seen to be filled with 'half-finished paintings.'[18] The narrator has been taken in a moment of vision into the indefinite world he fears; as a consequence his material surroundings have been miraculously transformed. But vision begins and ends in the imperfection of material life: the moment of vision, although eternal, is momentary. Man must return to the absurd material world. The indignant orthodox villagers who smash the spiritual mood and ceremony at the end of the story bring to mind the endings of some of Yeats's plays, *On Baile's Strand* and *The Death of Cuchulain* for example, where, suddenly after a spiritual image has been presented on the stage, the audience are consciously returned to the absurd material world from which the image blossomed. Having been carried to the very threshold of vision, the narrator of *Rosa Alchemica*, like many of the audience at the end of a play, seeks refuge in the 'only definite faith':[19]

> There are moments even now when I seem to hear those voices of exultation and lamentation, and when the indefinite world, which has but half lost its mastery over my heart and my intellect, seems about to claim a perfect mastery; but I carry the rosary about my neck, and when I hear, or seem to hear them, I press it to my heart and say, "He whose name is Legion is at our doors deceiving our intellects with subtlety and flattering our hearts with beauty, and we have no trust but in Thee"; and then the war that rages within me at other times is still, and I am at peace.[20]

II

Rosa Alchemica, *The Tables of the Law*, and *The Adoration of the Magi* explore the dilemma of characters caught between dream and vision, of characters who have renounced the joy of the mortal world but who have not been able to accept the tragic ecstasy of the immortal world to which they have half-awakened. In *The Tables of the Law*, Owen Aherne, like the narrator in *Rosa Alchemica*, has shut himself off from the material world and surrounded himself with works of art in the hope of achieving 'vision and ecstasy,' but until he adds to them English Pre-Raphaelite and French symbolist paintings he does not get beyond 'dreams of a curious and broken beauty.'[21] Owen Aherne has more capacity for vision than the narrator of *Rosa Alchemica* and is more capable of grasping the implications of the knowledge revealed to him; his inability, therefore, to live by the light of this knowledge has more tragic consequences.

He has the type of mind which 'when it has risen above, or is sunken below, the formalisms of half-education and the rationalisms of conventional affirmation and denial, turns away . . . from practicable desires and intuitions towards desires so unbounded that no human vessel can contain them, intuitions so immaterial that their sudden and far-off fire leaves heavy darkness about hand and foot.' For him the arts are not the dead mirrors of men's minds, but possess the power 'to overthrow nations, and finally life herself, by sowing everywhere unlimited desires, like torches thrown into a burning city.'[22] Aherne, consequently, can become for a time the revealer of the new dispensation, until the consciousness of his own mortality leads him to damnation and despair:

> What portion in the world can the artist have
> Who has awakened from the common dream
> But dissipation and despair?[23]

Like Hanrahan with his 'Book of the Great Dhoul' and Michael Robartes with his *Speculum Angelorum et Hominorum* (the Latin grammar was later corrected), Aherne has discovered a sacred book, Joachim of Flora's *Liber inducens in Evangelium aeternum*, which holds between its artistically decorated covers the annunciation of a new dispensation. The Kingdom of the Father, Aherne proclaims, has passed; the Kingdom of the Son is passing, and the Kingdom of the Spirit, the 'complete triumph of the Spirit . . . over the dead letter',[24] is yet to come. As one reads the passage in the sacred book that describes with delight the rejection of the repressive law of the Father one can understand why the young Joyce prized *The Tables of the Law* so highly.[25] While the rejection of the repressive commandments of the Father was perhaps within the comprehension of some of Yeats's readers in 1896, the sweeping away of the commandments of the Son must indeed have been startling: 'It is not necessary to judge every one by the law,' the narrator interjects, 'for we have also Christ's commandment of love':

> He turned and said, looking at me with shining eyes: "Jonathan Swift made a soul for the gentlemen of this city by hating his neighbour as himself."[26]

Whatever is in the soul, whether it be love or hate, must be expressed. The children of the Spirit must reveal the spirit hidden in the world, the 'divine ecstasy' and 'immortal fire' in every human passion, hope, desire and dream; they must reveal also the image of that ecstasy embodied in man and material nature:

> certain . . . were elected . . . to reveal that hidden substance of God which is colour and music and softness and a sweet odour; and that these have no father but the Holy Spirit. Just as poets and painters and musicians labour at their works, building them with lawless and lawful things alike, so long as they embody the beauty that is beyond the grave, these children of the Holy Spirit labour at their moments with eyes upon the shining substance on which Time has heaped the refuse of creation; for the world only exists to be a tale in the ears of coming generations; and terror and content, birth and death, love and hatred, and the fruit of the Tree, are but instruments for that supreme art which is to win us from life and gather us into eternity like doves into their dove-cots.[27]

The new revelation would elevate imagination and instinct, and preach that human life exists so that man may embody spirit. In articulating the spirit he embodies, man is gathered up into the artifice of eternity. Under the new dispensation the lives of men would be 'articulated and simplified as if seventy years were but one moment, or as if they were the leaping of a fish or the opening of a flower.'[28] The new dispensation, as revealed in *The Tables of the Law*, is the coming of the symbolic age, the revelation of the spirit embodied in all mortal forms.

But Catholicism seizes Aherne in 'the midst of the vertigo he called philosophy',[29] and holds him on the margin of the expression he knows to be possible. Earlier he had countered the orthodox objections of the narrator of *The Tables of the Law* by admitting the danger of the doctrines he preached: they implied the birth of the irrational and the violent disruption of the 'continuity and order' of the world; but man's desire for truth, Aherne contended at the time, is as instinctive as the moth's desire for light; therefore, complete freedom must be granted to the 'supreme art,' the revelation of the spirit embodied in the world, the 'art which is the foundation of all arts'.[30] Ten years later, when the narrator encounters him again, Aherne speaks of the 'extreme danger' and the 'boundless wickedness' the doctrines contain. He believes now that men's hearts 'perish every moment,' and because they perish 'God has made a simple and an arbitrary law that we may sin and repent'.[31] Men are mortal, and mortality to Aherne implies sin, the 'sense of separation' which is necessary before men can come to God. But because Aherne has discovered the law of his being, he cannot sin, as sin is commonly understood: he can only 'express or fail to express' his being; consequently, he feels he is damned forever:

> I am not among those for whom Christ died, and this is why I must be hidden. I have a leprosy that even eternity cannot cure. I have seen the whole, and how can I come again to believe that a part is the whole? I have lost my soul because I have looked out of the eyes of the angels.[32]

In a way this dilemma is expressed more sympathetically and more forcefully in the first version of the story in the *Savoy*:

"I am outside the salvation of Him who died for sinners, because I have lost the power of committing a sin. I found the secret law of my life, and, finding it, no longer desired to transgress, because it was my own law. Whatever my intellect and my soul commanded, I did, and sin passed from me, and I ceased to be among those for whom Christ died." And at the name of Christ he crossed himself with that involuntary gesture which marks those who have crossed themselves from childhood. "At first I tried to sin by breaking my law, although without desire; but the sin without desire is shadowy, like the sins of some phantom one has not visited even in dreams. You who are not lost, who may still speak to men and women, tell them that it is necessary to make an arbitrary law that one may be among those for whom Christ has died."

I went over and stood beside him, and said: "Prayer and penance will make you like other men."

"Not," he replied, "unless they can take from me my knowledge of the secret law."

A similar passage in *Autobiographies* suggests that Yeats may have had one of the Rhymers in mind as the prototype for Owen Aherne, possibly Lionel Johnson, for in the *Autobiographies* Yeats writes of Johnson and his friends:

> what can the Christian confessor say to those who more and more must make all out of the privacy of their thought, calling up perpetual images of desire, for he cannot say, "Cease to be an artist, cease to be a poet", where the whole life is art and poetry, nor can he bid men leave the world, who suffer from the terrors that pass before shut eyes.[33]

In 1898, also, Yeats concludes an article on Johnson by implying that he had 'renounced the joy of the world without accepting the joy of God',[34] which would leave him with the despair and damnation of Owen Aherne.

Aherne is caught in the irresolvable dilemma between instruction and instinct, between his orthodox Catholic teaching and the truth he has discovered in his own heart. What he does not realize is that instinct is a condition of truth, that mortality is a condition of immortality, that it is only by the recognition of the presence of the mortal and immortal elements in the vulnerable vessel called man that the apparently irresolvable paradox can be accepted.

III

The Adoration of the Magi announces the overthrow of the modern materialistic world and the return 'of the gods and the ancient things'.[35] Less is revealed, however, about the nature of the new dispensation than about the strange and unexpected manner of its coming. The Magi are three old men of the west of Ireland who because of their dedication to the 'heroic and simple' life have not fallen under the 'body and pressure' of modern times and can therefore understand instinctively the apocalyptic message that is revealed. They are sent to adore *not* the Christchild in the manger, but a dying harlot who has been chosen as the medium of the new annunciation because she has been rejected by the world: 'When the Immortals would overthrow the things that are to-day and bring the things that were yesterday, they have no one to help them, but one whom the things that are to-day have cast out.'[36] All 'follies' have gathered in the harlot's heart; 'all desires have awakened' in her body, and the flame in her breast, although malevolent in the eyes of the world, has not been quenched by prudence or practical law.

In the early versions of the story the harlot merely mentions the names of the Immortals, and this is sufficient to bring them again into the world. But in the more apocalyptic and forceful revised version the dying harlot gives birth not to a vulnerable child but to a unicorn, the creature which of all creatures is 'most unlike man . . . being cold, hard and virginal. It seemed to be born dancing; and was gone from the room wellnigh upon the instant, for it is of the nature of the unicorn to understand the shortness of life.'[37] The unicorn symbolizes spiritual energy and ecstatic joy, the opposite of the frailty characteristic of man and the material world.

The contrast presented in *The Adoration of the Magi* is between eternity and time, between virginal eternal forces and those things that have been corrupted by the world. Christianity, one of the old men concedes, may have been 'good' once, but it has become materialistic and secular:

> when people are good the world likes them and takes possession of them, and so eternity comes through people who are not good or who have been forgotten. Perhaps Christianity was good and the world liked it, so now it is going away and the Immortals are beginning to awake.[38]

The time is therefore imminent for the overthrow of a Christianity which has wooed and won the world.

In *Rosa Alchemica* and *The Tables of the Law* the narrators fear that all that bound them to spiritual and social order would be violently uprooted and their souls left 'naked and shivering among the winds that blow from beyond this world and from beyond the stars';[39] consequently they turn at the end of the stories to what is familiar and certain, the one 'definite faith'.[40] So, too, at the end of *The Adoration of the Magi* the narrator resolves to lose himself 'among the prayers and the sorrows of the multitude', to turn 'into a pathway' which will lead him from the Immortals and 'from the Order of the Alchemical Rose.'[41] One can sense the wry humour and irony with which these characters have been conceived, and what clings in the mind is not the orthodox objections of the narrators, but the apocalyptic annunciation of a new dispensation, a message miraculously revealed by characters who, as Yeats writes later, 'become a part of the phantasmagoria through which I can alone express my convictions about the world.'[42]

IV SOME IMPLICATIONS OF THE SYMBOLIC APPROACH:
The Wind Among the Reeds

This sense of symbolic apocalypse dominates Yeats's work during the eighteen-nineties, and indeed one of the implications of symbolism as far as Yeats is concerned is a sense of apocalypse. The position of the symbolist is a precarious one, because he can easily be led from the 'half-lights' which glimmer from symbol to symbol to a world of pure essences, of 'impossible purities';[1] he can easily be led from the spirituality that material forms embody to the point where he loses all consciousness of the form itself, where 'so august a beauty' moves before his mind that he forgets the things that move before his eyes.[2] Perhaps it is well, Yeats argues, that few believe in the things of eternity, for if many did, men would turn from 'parliaments and universities and libraries and run into the wilderness to so waste the body, and to so hush the unquiet mind that, still living, they might pass the doors the dead pass daily; for who among the wise would trouble himself with making laws or in writing history or in weighing the earth if the things of eternity seemed ready at hand?'[3]

In the mind of the symbolist, Yeats argues, the 'Last Judgment has already begun'.[4] For one implication of the artist's awareness of the things of eternity, and of his ability to evoke them in symbols, is his desire for the apocalyptic destruction of the material world so that he can be consumed into the ideal beauty he seeks. It is this implication that Yeats explores in *The Wind Among the Reeds*.[5]

The title of the volume is significant. In a note to the first edition Yeats indicates that he used the wind 'as a symbol of vague desires and hopes, not merely because the Sidhe are in the wind, or because the wind bloweth as it listeth, but because **wind and spirit and vague desire have been associated everywhere.**'[6] At the head of his hierarchy of perfect images, he explains in 1894, is 'a certain night scene long ago, when I heard the wind blowing in a bed of reeds by the border of a little lake.'[7] He associates the scene with the 'inmost voice of Celtic sadness, and of Celtic longing for infinite things the world has never seen.'[8] The fragile body when stirred by spiritual longing becomes like a 'wind-blown reed';[9] conversely the lamentation of the Sidhe over the fallen material world is expressed in the 'lamentation of the wind-tossed reeds'.[10] The wind among the reeds then becomes a symbol of the spirit stirring the human heart, with longing and lamentation, with lamentation over an imperfect material world, with longing for a perfect spiritual world.

Earlier, during the eighteen-nineties, Yeats had asserted that eternal beauty could be found in the 'foolish' ephemeral forms of nature:

> *Come near, that no more blinded by man's fate,*
> *I find under the boughs of love and hate,*
> *In all poor foolish things that live a day,*
> *Eternal beauty wandering on her way.*[11]

Yeats invokes the proud and passionate beauty manifested in Irish legend and tradition to inspire his poetry. He struggles, however, to maintain his own identity, to remain in conscious control, lest overcome by the ideal beauty he invokes and serves, he would no longer retain contact with the definite world but be spirited away to a world of pure essence:

> *Come near, come near, come near — Ah, leave me still*
> *A little space for the rose-breath to fill!*
> *Lest I no more hear common things that crave;*
> *The weak worm hiding down in its small cave,*
> *The field-mouse running by me in the grass,*
> *And heavy mortal hopes that toil and pass;*
> *But seek alone to hear the strange things said*
> *By God to the bright hearts of those long dead,*
> *And learn to chaunt a tongue men do not know.*

The title of the poem, 'To the Rose upon the Rood of Time', suggests that ideal beauty, 'grown sad with its eternity,' needs the material world to be fulfilled. Once manifested in time, however, Beauty must suffer until, like the body of Christ, it is dramatically cast off on the cross.

The Rose, as we know, is one of Yeats's central symbols during the eighteen-nineties. It is a symbol of the physical and spiritual beauty manifested in tribal tradition, in nature, art, and in certain women. Some of the Rose poems imagine Eternal Beauty 'as suffering with man',[12] while others emphasize the secret, mysterious, and almost unattainable qualities of the Rose. In 'The Secret Rose' the great leaves of the inviolate Rose encompass all the wisdom, beauty, and valour of ancient Ireland. In 'The Rose of the World' the beauty manifested in the 'red lips' of Helen and Deirdre stirs men to service and sacrifice: so uncompromising and intense is their passion for the possession of the beauty to which they have awakened that it results in the destruction of the mundane world, in the death of the sons of Usna and the destruction of Troy. The lips are mournful because men are no longer willing to give such signs of service:

> Who dreamed that beauty passes like a dream?
> For these red lips, with all their mournful pride,
> Mournful that no new wonder may betide,
> Troy passed away in one high funeral gleam,
> And Usna's children died.
>
> We and the labouring world are passing by:
> Amid men's souls, that waver and give place
> Like the pale waters in their wintry race,
> Under the passing stars, foam of the sky,
> Lives on this lonely face.

It is not Beauty, but men and the labouring world, who pass 'like a dream'.

The pattern that can be traced in Yeats's prose during the eighteen-nineties can also be traced in his poetry. From a recognition of eternal beauty in the ephemeral forms of nature he quickly passes to an alchemical dream and thence to a state of vision where he receives inspiration directly from the invisible spiritual world. In 'The Lover Tells of the Rose in His Heart', for example, he no longer sees eternal beauty in 'all poor foolish things that live a day,' but the material world, having become separated from the spiritual, is now seen as uncomely and broken, as wronging the image of his beloved which arouses in the depths of his sorrowing heart a thirst for ideal beauty. Like the narrator in *Rosa Alchemica*, he hungers to transmute the material world into a dead perfection, a 'casket of gold', which is more permanent than the things it contains. Like the narrator of *Rosa Alchemica*, the poet is caught in a sterile state of alchemical dream. He is soon, however, to be swept away into the immaterial world that the narrator of *Rosa Alchemica* fears, as he hears and responds to the call of the supernatural Sidhe who, according to Yeats, carry out the will of Ideal Beauty:[13]

> *Away, come away:*
> *Empty your heart of its mortal dream.*
> *The winds awaken, the leaves whirl round,*
> *Our cheeks are pale, our hair is unbound,*
> *Our breasts are heaving, our eyes are agleam,*
> *Our arms are waving, our lips are apart;*
> *And if any gaze on our rushing band,*
> *We come between him and the deed of his hand,*
> *We come between him and the hope of his heart.*
> *The host is rushing 'twixt night and day,*
> *And where is there hope or deed as fair?*

Unlike the poet in 'To the Rose upon the Rood of Time', who consciously invokes ideal beauty to come to him, the poet here is no longer in control. No longer individual and indissoluble, he becomes, like the narrator of *Rosa Alchemica*, passive and potentially a medium for the expression of indefinite spiritual impulses. Once awakened to the spiritual world, he grows indifferent to mundane things: for him no mortal hope or deed is as 'fair' as the response to the call of the Sidhe.

These are the implications which *The Wind Among the Reeds* explores: the separation of material and spiritual; the tension between the broken world we perceive with our senses and the ideal world we are capable of apprehending with our imaginations. 'Into the Twilight' calls the heart from the materialistic 'nets of wrong and right' into a world where spiritual essences still haunt material forms:

> Come, heart, where hill is heaped upon hill:
> For there the mystical brotherhood
> Of sun and moon and hollow and wood
> And river and stream work out their will. . . .

'The Moods' presents the contrast between the permanence of spiritual moods and the impermanence of material manifestations of the mood. 'The Unappeasable Host' contrasts the fate of the human child and the children of the Tuatha De Danaan. For the Danaan children there are 'cradles of wrought gold' and the exhilaration of unconfined spirit, but for the human child there is only the cradle of suffering, the confinement of the narrow grave, the uneasy tension between the conventional religion one knows and the unconventional longing one fears:

> O heart the winds have shaken, the unappeasable host
> Is comelier than candles at Mother Mary's feet.

Some of the poems of *The Wind Among the Reeds* achieve the balanced harmony of some of the Rose poems. The beloved is imagined as the embodiment of ideal beauty; the poet recognizes that ideal beauty is unattainable for man in his present sphere of existence, or is attainable only during the miraculous moment of vision which precedes artistic creation; he knows consequently that he must be content with the *search* for the ideal, with offering up the myrrh and frankincense of his own poetry to the beauty he believes to exist:

> I bring you with reverent hands
> The books of my numberless dreams,
> White woman that passion has worn
> As the tide wears the dove-grey sands,
> And with heart more old than the horn
> That is brimmed from the pale fire of time:
> White woman with numberless dreams,
> I bring you my passionate rhyme.

Through the beloved the poet makes contact with the beauty which existed before man fell a slave to the external world. As a consequence, the forces of mortality are momentarily held at bay:

> Beloved, let your eyes half close, and your heart beat
> Over my heart, and your hair fall over my breast,
> Drowning love's lonely hour in deep twilight of rest,
> And hiding their tossing manes and their tumultuous feet.

The hair and eyes of the beloved are emphasized. Hair is a perfect symbol, because whatever conceals a spiritual essence may also be the means through which it is revealed. The eyes of the beloved are half-closed to suggest a trance-like timeless ecstasy, to suggest complete absorption in an inner reality. The beloved is oblivious to the external world: her heart is full of its own sweetness and under her half-closed eyelids 'even longing drowns under its own excess'.[14]

But the identification which the aesthetic desires of the poet force between the physical beloved and an impossible ideal can be as agonizing as it is imaginatively fulfilling. Once the beloved is imagined as the embodiment of ideal beauty, as in 'The Lover Mourns for the Loss of Love', or once the beloved is spirited away to an ideal world, as in 'The Host of the Air', physical fulfilment becomes impossible. For the poet who remains in the mundane world the sadness and forced gaiety of his own poetry is sometimes only a hollow compensation for what he has lost through the power of his own imagination.

In *The Wind Among the Reeds* the call of the spiritual is symbolized by the tide upon the shore, the call of birds, and, more significantly, by the cry of the wind: 'Have you not heard', Yeats writes in 'The Everlasting Voices',

> that our hearts are old,
> That you call in birds, in wind on the hill,
> In shaken boughs, in tide on the shore?

Like all symbols, however, the wind has dual aspects. For what awakens man's thirst for spiritual perfection also awakens his consciousness of the imperfection of the material world. Several poems in the volume present the anguished cry of characters who claim that the stirring of the wind is a curse rather than a blessing. To Hanrahan in 'He Reproves the Curlew' the cry of the curlew or the wind is resented because it tortures his mind with the memory of the beauty he has lost:

> O curlew, cry no more in the air,
> Or only to the water in the West;
> Because your crying brings to my mind
> Passion-dimmed eyes and long heavy hair
> That was shaken out over my breast:
> There is enough evil in the crying of wind.

In 'He Thinks of His Past Greatness when a Part of the Constellations of Heaven' Mongan articulates the curse of mortality and consciousness: the beasts of the wilderness and birds of the air can find completion in their inarticulate state, but man's consciousness of his own mortality comes between him and the impossible spiritual fulfilment he craves:

> I became a man, a hater of the wind,
> Knowing one, out of all things, alone, that his head
> May not lie on the breast nor his lips on the hair
> Of the woman that he loves, until he dies.
> O beast of the wilderness, bird of the air,
> Must I endure your amorous cries? [15]

Mongan is the persona Yeats uses in *The Wind Among the Reeds* to represent a character whose thirst for the spiritual is so intense that he desires either the destruction of the mundane world or the cessation of the cry of the spiritual.

The themes we have been treating in *The Wind Among the Reeds* converge and are pressed beyond their rational conclusion in 'He Mourns for the Change that has Come upon Him and His Beloved, and Longs for the End of the World':

> Do you not hear me calling, white deer with no horns?
> I have been changed to a hound with one red ear;
> I have been in the Path of Stones and the Wood of Thorns,
> For somebody hid hatred and hope and desire and fear
> Under my feet that they follow you night and day.
> A man with a hazel wand came without sound;
> He changed me suddenly; I was looking another way;
> And now my calling is but the calling of a hound;
> And Time and Birth and Change are hurrying by.

The ideal and man's passion for the ideal are depicted in terms of the frantic pursuit of the deer by the hound; and deer and hound, Yeats explains in his Notes to the poem, are 'Irish symbols of the desire of the man which is for the woman, and the desire of the woman which is for the desire of the man'.[16] In other words, the desire of man is for the ideal, and the desire of the ideal is for the desire of man; the implication is that no harmony can be achieved between the two in a mortal passing world. Yeats had written about the self-created hell of the artist who seeks ideal beauty with too avid a thirst in *The Celtic Twilight*:

> One day I saw faintly an immense pit of blackness, round which went a circular parapet, and on this parapet sat innumerable apes eating precious stones out of the palms of their hands. The stones glittered green and crimson, and the apes devoured them with an insatiable hunger. I knew that I saw my own Hell there, the Hell of the artist, and that all who sought after beautiful and wonderful things with too avid a thirst, lost peace and form and became shapeless and common.[17]

Four years after this realization the poet views the material world as the way in which a spiritual essence is concealed rather than revealed; consequently, he hungers for the appearance of the rough mythological beast which will destroy the manifest world, now conceived as the enemy of imagination and the ideal:

> I would that the Boar without bristles had come from the West
> And had rooted the sun and moon and stars out of the sky
> And lay in the darkness, grunting, and turning to his rest.

Similarly, in 'Hanrahan Laments because of His Wanderings', the insatiable passion for the ideal leads Hanrahan to thirst for the violent destruction of the material world; in this poem, however, the apocalyptic agent is not the 'Boar without bristles' but the 'death-pale deer':

> I would that the death-pale deer
> Had come through the mountain side,
> And trampled the mountain away,
> And drunk up the murmuring tide;
> For the winds that awakened the stars
> Are blowing through my blood....[18]

The most forceful apocalyptic poem in *The Wind Among the Reeds* is 'The Valley of the Black Pig':

> The dews drop slowly and dreams gather: unknown spears
> Suddenly hurtle before my dream-awakened eyes,
> And then the clash of fallen horsemen and the cries
> Of unknown perishing armies beat about my ears.
> We who still labour by the cromlech on the shore,
> The grey cairn on the hill, when day sinks drowned in dew,
> Being weary of the world's empires, bow down to you,
> Master of the still stars and of the flaming door.

This poem presents the contrast between the fate of those who serve the temporal world and the still self-sufficiency of artists who, 'weary of the world's empires,' bow in solitude to the author of eternity, the 'Master of the still stars and of the flaming door.' It is to be noted that the stars are not the changing stars of nature, but the *still* stars of eternity: 'A starlit or a moonlit dome disdains / All that man is,' Yeats writes in 'Byzantium', but thirty years before writing these lines, during the eighteen-nineties, he had associated the still stars with the 'ideal world' which is created by the imagination, the 'world of the dead'.[19]

The Wind Among the Reeds takes Yeats beyond the threshold of apocalypse. Suddenly in a dark materialistic age the spirit, symbolized by the wind, stirs the fragile human heart, symbolized by a reed, with spiritual longing, awakening it to an ideal world, but at the same time impressing on it the indignities and inadequacies of the material world. The heart, forgetting that mortality is a condition of immortality, is caught in uneasy tension between what it desires and what is not possible as long as it retains its humanity. It is led finally to the impossible purity of the spiritual ideal to which it has awakened, and it awaits without ambivalence the darkening of the flickering stars. It cries out for the destruction of the material forms which, paradoxically, embody the spiritual essence it craves but with which it can no longer be content:

> I, too, await
> The hour of thy great wind of love and hate.

> When shall the stars be blown about the sky,
> Like the sparks blown out of a smithy, and die?
> Surely thine hour has come, thy great wind blows,
> Far-off, most secret, and inviolate Rose?

Yeats's apocalyptic symbols in *The Wind Among the Reeds* are the death-pale deer and, more importantly, the Black Pig. What these symbols signify in the poems is clear enough, but Yeats's prose explanations of their meaning often lead to confusion and apparent contradiction. The meaning of the apocalyptic symbols is further complicated by their use in Irish folklore and legend. In 1856, for example, Nicholas O'Kearney mentioned a folk belief that 'a massacre . . . shall be perpetrated upon the mass of the Catholic population of Ulster by their Protestant neighbours, in . . . the Valley of the Black Pig'.[20] Some years later the poet and antiquary Samuel Ferguson wrote that the Black Pig was 'a mythical monster, said to have been banished, after the establishment of Christianity, to the Hebridean seas, where his "rootings" may be seen in stormy weather in the hollows of the waves, and his "gruntings" heard from the caverned rocks'.[21] Another folk belief concerning the Black Pig, originating, perhaps, in written tradition with John O'Donovan, is recorded by R. S. Rogers: a certain schoolmaster was in the habit of changing his pupils into hounds and one into a hare; on learning this the father of the boy changed into a hare went to the master:

> "is it true that you can do these things?" And he said he could, so he says, "change yourself now into a pig." So the master turned himself into a pig, and the man took the book, and the master was in the form of a pig and he couldn't take it from him and he burned it in the fire. So the pig lost his senses altogether when he saw this and he ran through the country tearing up the land as he went. And somewhere in the neighbourhood of Tullaghan he ran into the sea and was drowned.[22]

Before the Civil War the Black Pig was reputed to have appeared in County Roscommon, but although visible only to children, its appearance, *The Irish Times* proclaimed, portended 'serious trouble in Ireland . . . and legends relate that all along the north of the B.P. there will be awful slaughter of the Irish race.'[23]

That Yeats was familiar with some of these traditions is certain. The conclusion of 'He Mourns for the Change that has Come upon Him and His Beloved, and Longs for the End of the World', for example, incorporates some of the phraseology Ferguson had used in describing the beast. In *The Celtic Twilight,* too, Yeats alludes to the folk belief that the Battle of the Black Pig is 'a battle between Ireland and England'; to him, however, it is 'an Armageddon which shall quench all things in the Ancestral Darkness again'.[24] For what was regarded with ambivalence and fear by the folk was welcomed by the prophetic poet. The Pig and the death-pale deer become to him symbols 'of the end of all things',[25] 'fragments of ancestral darkness' which 'will overthrow the world.'[26]

At certain points in his prose Yeats makes it clear that this apocalyptic destruction is to be desired. 'The Irish peasantry', he writes in 1896, 'have for generations comforted themselves, in their misfortunes, with visions of a great battle, to be fought in a mysterious valley called "The Valley of the Black Pig," and to break at last the power of their enemies.'[27] Three years later he writes: 'All over Ireland there are prophecies of the coming rout of the enemies of Ireland, in a certain Valley of the Black Pig'.[28] During the eighteen-nineties Yeats associates Ireland with the imagination and the ideal, and therefore in the Battle of the Black Pig the enemies of imagination and the ideal would be annihilated. The passion for the ideal and the desire to dissipate the darkness of the material world are, Yeats indicates, one and the same.[29] For when man is capable of visualizing the 'death-pale deer', Yeats explains in *Ideas of Good and Evil,* he is coming 'out of the darkness and passion of the world into some day of partial regeneration'.[30]

At other points in his prose, however, Yeats's explanation of the meaning of his apocalyptic symbols is less clear:

> The pig seems to have been originally a genius of the corn, and, seemingly because the too great power of their divinity makes divine things dangerous to mortals, its flesh was forbidden to many eastern nations; but as the meaning of the prohibition was forgotten, abhorrence took the place of reverence, pigs and boars grew into types of evil, and were described

as the enemies of the very gods they once typified. . . . The Pig would, therefore, become the Black Pig, a type of cold and of winter that awake in November, the old beginning of winter, to do battle with the summer, and with the fruit and leaves, and finally, as I suggest; and as I believe, for the purposes of poetry; of the darkness that will at last destroy the gods and the world.[31]

This was written in 1899, but in 1908 Yeats compressed the note to: 'the battle is mythological, and . . . the Pig it is named from must be a type of cold and winter doing battle with the summer, or of death battling with life. For the purposes of poetry, at any rate, I think it is a symbol of the darkness that will destroy the world.'[32] As one reads these notes, however, one must remember that in the world of the Sidhe the seasons are reversed, that when winter and darkness descend on our world, summer and the light of imagination are awakening in the spiritual world.

Yeats associates the Battle of the Black Pig with a former mythological battle, the Battle of Moytura, fought between the Tuatha De Danaan, 'the powers of light, and warmth, and fruitfulness, and goodness,' and the Formorians, 'the powers of darkness, and cold, and barrenness, and badness'. The victory of the Tuatha De Danaan over the Formorians in this battle, Yeats claims, led to the 'establishment of the habitable world, the rout of ancestral darkness'.[33] When the habitable world was first established, however, spiritual essences and material forms were united. The material world was haunted and holy. But later essence and form, meaning and symbol, separated, and the manifest world which once embodied spiritual essences is now regarded as the enemy of spirituality. It is consequently to be destroyed in the Battle of the Black Pig; and continuing the analogy which Yeats suggests with the Battle of Moytura, the manifest world seems now to be associated with the Formorians, and those who defeat the world, or remain oblivious to it, as in Yeats's poem 'The Valley of the Black Pig', seem to be associated with the Tuatha De Danaan, the powers of light and the imagination.

But Yeats only hints at this identification: the most he says is that these battles are 'the battle of all things with shadowy decay.'[34] It seems as if he wished to remain intentionally vague in his prose explanations of what he had made clear in his poems. Only once does he indicate in his prose what would replace the manifest world once the great battle was over: the ancient divinities, he indicates vaguely, would be free once more to set up 'their temples of grey stone.'[35]

Through the phantasmagorical characters of *Rosa Alchemica* and *The Tables of the Law*, Robartes and Aherne, Yeats could be explicit as to the nature of the new dispensation and yet balance his ambivalence towards its implications by the orthodox objections of the narrator. But in the poems of *The Wind Among the Reeds* he is led slowly and logically to the point where the destruction of the mundane world is imminent and desired. His faith in the existence of the ideal and his realization of the impossibility of attaining it as long as man is burdened with a broken bewildering body leads him to believe that the ideal can be achieved only when the light of the manifest world has been snuffed out. Rationally he is led into the irrational, into the unknown, into the darkness he wishes to see descend upon the world. The poems seem to indicate that this surrender to the unknown is necessary before man can be freed from dependence on the material world. The apocalyptic symbols are terrifying, however, because man is reluctant to relinquish his grasp on familiar forms, and because the poet, his prophetic eyes fixed only on the act of destruction, does not indicate what is to replace the material world. *The Wind Among the Reeds* takes a prophetic leap into the dark; the rest, for Yeats at least, is an act of faith and surrender.

But the position is an impossible one. Without an imperfect material world there can be no thirst for spiritual perfection, no opportunity for the agony of the human heart to be expressed. In *The Wind Among the Reeds*, therefore, Yeats is led beyond the symbolic approach, for the true symbolist must convey man's sense of frailty as well as his thirst for perfection, his vulnerability as well as his vision. The true symbolist must preserve the precarious balance between form and spirit, one of which is as significant as the other, and always at his back he hears the cry of a bird, or the wind, or the tide, signifying that spiritual essences need material forms to become embodied and so fulfilled.

V A BEAST AND A UNICORN:

Where There is Nothing and *The Unicorn from the Stars*

I

Apart from the apocalyptic beast and the death-pale deer, the significant symbols in the volume we have been analysing were the wind blowing among the reeds, the cry of the birds, and the tide washing the innumerable dove-grey sands upon the shore. These, as we have seen, were symbols of eternal spirit stirring the fragile human being with longing and lamentation, with longing for the perfect spiritual world the heart desires and lamentation over the imperfect material world it inhabits. In *Where There is Nothing*, the play which takes the thought of *The Wind Among the Reeds* to its point of disintegration, these symbols of man's vision and vulnerability figure only fleetingly:

FATHER ALOYSIUS . . . Do you hear the curlews calling; they make me sad.

FATHER BARTLEY They make me sad, too.

PAUL Those sad cries are God lamenting over the fall of man, but it is better to listen to His rejoicings when a soul ascends into heaven. The crows are my darlings! I like their harsh merriment better than those sad cries. I often saw them coming home in a storm when I was a child, whirling hither and thither, drunk with the wind, crying out to one another as the witches do when their white horses dance upon the clouds.

FATHER BARTLEY What a great noise the wind made last night. I wonder it did not tear away the whole roof, instead of this little corner.

PAUL That is a good noise, too. The wind tears down everything before it trying to get back to the place it came from.[1]

In *Where There is Nothing* the symbols of lamentation which had featured prominently in *The Wind Among the Reeds* — the wind, the tide, and the cries of birds — give place to the more apocalyptic symbols of destruction which had also featured in the volume, the beast and the unicorn, developments of the Black Pig and the death-pale deer.

Where There is Nothing begins where *The Wind Among the Reeds* ended. In *The Wind Among the Reeds* the apocalyptic beast that the poet desired to destroy the enemies of imagination and the ideal seemed remote and mysterious, seemed something that was to come from *beyond* the world. But in *Where There is Nothing* the rough beast is brought into close contact with humanity and is closely identified with the central character of the play, Paul Ruttledge:

> Sometimes I dream I am pulling down my own house, and sometimes it is the whole world that I am pulling down. I would like to have great iron claws, and to put them about the pillars, and to pull and pull till everything fell into pieces.[2]

At some points in the play there is a definite suggestion that the beast is within the human breast itself, waiting to be released. But at other points dramatic considerations demand that the beast be seen as something to be pursued; still, however, it is identified with the central character:

> there is a wild beast I would overtake. . . . [I]t's a very terrible wild beast, with iron teeth and brazen claws that can root up spires and towers. . . . My wild beast is Laughter, the mightiest of the enemies of God. I will outrun it and make it friendly.[3]

The beast, with its hard cold sapphire eyes, its iron teeth, and brazen wings and claws, can 'overturn governments, and all settled order',[4] and 'bring back the old joyful, dangerous, individual life.'[5] This is the 'brazen winged beast' which Yeats associates with 'laughing, ecstatic destruction', the beast which he says himself he 'afterwards described in my poem "The Second Coming" '.[6] In *Where There is Nothing* it is symbolic of the creative joy that mocks 'death and oblivion',[7] that shatters the dead self-imposed order of the world.

Where There is Nothing is, Yeats admits, 'loosely constructed', but he was attempting to discover 'if a play would keep its unity upon the stage with no other device than one always dominant person about whom the world was always drifting away.'[8] Paul Ruttledge, the character about whom the play is centred, revolts against the utilitarianism, the vested interests, ulterior motives, generalized activities, self-adulation, routine, boring impositions and responsibilities forced on him by his materialistic friends. These people, who measure success by the number of societies a man has joined, have never had a 'dangerous thought'; consequently Paul represents them in terms of tamed farmyard creatures. On the other hand, he envisions himself as an animal 'of the wild sort.' He wants to 'get drunk in, to drink contentedly out of the cup of life, out of the drunken cup of life',[9] to 'rejoice without ceasing, although the world shudder at my joy.'[10] He desires, in short, the freedom that society cannot give, to express the impulses of his heart, to live unconstrained by law or custom. Consequently he rejects formalized society and turns, dramatically, to the roads:

> I want to be a vagabond, a wanderer. . . . Did you ever think that the roads are the only things that are endless; that one can walk on and on and on, and never be stopped by a gate or a wall? They are the serpent of eternity. I wonder they have never been worshipped. What are the stars beside them? They never meet one another. The roads are the only things that are infinite. They are all endless.[11]

Wanderers possess, Paul maintains, individuality and self-reliance; their spirit has not been broken by routine responsibilities, and like the saints of olden times they consider the world as their enemy: 'These men fight in their way as your saints fought, for their hand is against the world. I want the happiness of men who fight, who are hit and hit back, not the fighting of men in red coats, that formal, soon-finished fighting, but the endless battle, the endless battle.'[12]

Where There is Nothing explores ways of destroying a world which, having grown old, is regarded as the enemy of instinct. Paul begins by attempting to shock his friends, by attempting to expose the sterility and implicit hypocrisy of the world in which his neighbours wallow. He changes clothes with the tinkers, becomes a vagabond, and with sudden disdain for sobriety and morality fills his fellow vagabonds with drink so that they would taste the type of joy, ecstasy, and 'drunkenness' that he claims is reserved for them in Heaven. He conducts a mock trial to show that his friends are blind hypocrites, not the Christians they profess to be. But this method of overthrowing the order of the world, this direct satiric method, is for Paul, as for Yeats, a false one. Satire implies the reality of an external object. With the satiric approach one's eyes must remain focused on the world which, the symbolist argues, one must reject or at least become indifferent to. Paul begins the play by attempting to punish society; at the end of Act III, however, he realizes that he can and must punish nobody but himself.

Act IV initiates a new mood and explores another way of shattering the order of the material world. There is too a dramatic change in the symbolism by which the mood is expressed. The apocalyptic agent becomes now not the brazen winged beast but the unicorn:

> I saw a great many angels riding upon unicorns, white angels on white unicorns. They all stood round me, and they cried out, "Brother Paul, go and preach; get up and preach, Brother Paul." And then they laughed aloud, and the unicorns trampled the ground as though the world were already falling in pieces.[13]

The unicorn, the creature which is 'most unlike man of all living things,'[14] symbolizes ecstatic joy and spiritual energy, 'virginal strength, a rushing, lasting, tireless strength',[15] the opposite of the frailty characteristic of man and the material world.

For the wild excess, drunkenness, and open defiance of the law, for the direct assault upon social manners which Paul had advocated in the first three acts of the play he substitutes in the fourth act mortification of the flesh, meditation, and preaching. By meditation, by fixing the mind on 'one joyful thought', it is released from 'the wandering of nature' and is brought to the threshold of trance; a powerful light gathers as it receives from the disembodied soul of the universe, from *Anima Mundi*, a spiritual image. Trance, Paul preaches, takes the mind beyond 'law and number', beyond time and into eternity: men become the medium for eternal truths and at the same time learn mastery over their own souls:

> I prayed and fasted till at last one night in my cell a sudden light enfolded me, and I had thoughts that were not thoughts, I seemed to rise above law and number. I became king and priest in my own house, and learned, I know not how, the meditations that liberate the soul and unite it to the lawless unity.[16]

Paul has become a Friar, and to some of his fellow Friars his teaching is, of course, heresy: 'entire submission' is the only thing the Superior of the order will accept. To preach that 'the kingdom of heaven is within',[17] that man can be master of his own soul, one orthodox Friar proclaims, is 'against the order of nature'; for Paul, however, religion must be 'wholly supernatural, . . . so opposed to the order of nature that the world can never capture it.' Supernatural truth defies natural order, and if man has become the medium for supernatural truths he must, without regard to punishment or consequence, 'tell them at once before they slip away'.[18] Despite the warnings of his friends, therefore, Paul reveals the truths that have come to him in vision.

Paul's sermon, the part of the play which caused most difficulty, summarizes the thought Yeats had articulated in his poems, stories, and critical prose during the eighteen-nineties. When the world was created, Paul explains, the earth was seen as the expression of the 'Love of God'; men were filled with the 'Will of God' and acted according to the impulse of their hearts. But later, men, choosing to be secure rather than blessed, created law and in the process enslaved their hearts to an external reality: the 'Laws were the first sin. They were the first mouthful of the apple, the moment man made them he began to die'. God had 'put holiness into everything' he created: 'everything that desires is full of His Will, and everything that is beautiful is full of His Love', but men, by proclaiming that only one building, the Church, and only one day of the week, the Sabbath, was holy, put limitations on God's holiness.[19]

Sin and death, Paul contends, 'came into the world the day Newton eat the apple.'[20] In other words, when man subjected his soul to the external world, and began to study the world for its own sake, he fell: 'the embrace that was to have been eternal ended, lips and hands were parted.'[21] Consequently, all laws, churches, even the world itself must be destroyed, for where there is nothing, where the light of sense and the material world has been snuffed out, there, for Paul as for Yeats, is God:

> The Christian's business is not reformation but revelation, and the only labours he can put his hand to can never be accomplished in Time. He must so live that all things shall pass away. . . . We must become blind, and deaf, and dizzy. We must get rid of everything that is not measureless eternal life. We must put out hope as I put out this candle. . . . And memory as I put out this candle. . . . And thought, the waster of Life, as I put out this candle. . . . And at last we must put out the light of the Sun and of the Moon, and all the light of the World and the World itself. . . . We must destroy the World; we must destroy everything that has Law and Number, for where there is nothing, there is God. . . . [Y]ou cannot silence my thoughts. I learned them from Jesus Christ, who made a terrible joy, and sent it to overturn governments, and all settled order.[22]

This sermon, of course, results in Paul's banishment from the Friary, but he takes with him several of the monks who have been converted to the new doctrine. The monks, however, find it more difficult to preach in the world than in the monastery: in the monastery they could offer 'absolution here, and heaven after', but in the world they find that people are so involved with their own mortal troubles, with sickness, sin, and death, that they do not take readily to the doctrine that 'the kingdom of heaven is within'.[23] Disillusioned, therefore, with the indifference with which their message is received, and also with the practical discomforts they experience in the world, the monks decide to gather an army to fight the new battle. At first Paul is attracted by the idea:

> We could march on the towns, and we could break up all settled order; we could bring back the old joyful, dangerous, individual life. . . . We will have one great banner that will go in front, it will take two men to carry it, and on it we will have Laughter, with his iron claws and his wings of brass and his eyes like sapphires. . . .[24]

But armies, Paul quickly realizes, involve organization, 'law and number'. Armies belong to history and time; the old order may be destroyed, but what would replace it would not differ in essentials from what had been destroyed. The battle, therefore, is not external, but internal, one which each individual has to fight and win for himself:

> I was forgetting, we cannot destroy the world with armies, it is inside our minds that it must be destroyed, it must be consumed in a moment inside our minds. God will accomplish his last judgment, first in one man's mind and then in another. He is always planning last judgments. And yet it takes a long time, and that is why he laments in the wind and in the reeds and in the cries of the curlews.[25]

Paul at this point has gone beyond concern with social mores, beyond armies, beyond even a desire to preach. It is enough, he claims at the end of the play, to be 'a witness for the truth'.[26] Thus the way in which the material world is to be defeated has developed from the point in *The Wind Among the Reeds* where the apocalyptic agent was mythological and from beyond the world to the point in *Where There is Nothing* where the apocalyptic agent is identified with a human character, and this character is made to realize that the battle between spiritual and material is not physical but mental, and is won or lost in the mind of each individual.

Where There is Nothing concludes, as *Rosa Alchemica* had concluded, with a village riot against the disciples of the new doctrine, as the mob attempt to smash whatever threatens familiar forms. This conclusion, like the conclusions to so many of Yeats's plays, signifies the never-ceasing tension between material and spiritual, and signifies also that all spiritual endeavours begin and end in the absurdity of mortal life. Mortal death, the fate feared by those who live solely for the senses and the body, is welcomed, however, by those whose mental eyes have been awakened to the spiritual truth and beauty that lie beyond the world and for which they can become a medium during their mortal lives: 'Death is the last adventure, the first perfect joy, for at death the soul comes into possession of itself, and returns to the joy that made it.'[27]

II

In *The Wind Among the Reeds* and in the early acts of *Where There is Nothing* Yeats had worked himself into a position from which there was no easy escape. This thought had led him to the conclusion that the apocalyptic destruction of the material world was necessary and imminent. But whether the apocalyptic agent was from beyond mankind, as in *The Wind Among the Reeds*, or whether it was closely identified with a human character, as in *Where There is Nothing*, Yeats seemed to realize in 1902 that the destruction of the world was impossible by direct physical action. Yeats as a symbolist must also have realized that the material world was as necessary as the spiritual: without an imperfect material world there could be no desire for spiritual perfection, no opportunity for the agony of the human heart to be expressed. The situation in *Where There is Nothing*, too, lacked dramatic force, for no matter how impressive the philosophy may seem, the creator of such thought ran the risk of appearing a Quixote eternally tilting at impossible mills.

The conclusion Paul reaches in the fifth act of *Where There is Nothing*, that the battle is internal rather than external, points towards the resolution of the impossible situation. But the realization came too late to balance Paul's direct assault on social decorum during the first three acts of the play, and his proselytizing attempts to convert the world during the last two acts. *Where There is Nothing* was therefore in obvious need of revision before it was passed for the press, but Yeats, having written the play in a fortnight in order to prevent George Moore from plagiarizing the plot, was anxious to have it published as soon as possible.[28] The play, first published in 1902, went through three substantially-revised editions within a year. But Yeats quickly tired of its structure and its central character. It had been too hastily written; its movement was too hurried and violent. Also, as Yeats points out later, while a 'dominating' character may increase 'dramatic effect in a superficial way',[29] for the same character to set out 'at once lightly and confidently to overthrow the order of the world' alienates an audience's sympathy.[30] If the character had spoken with 'humility', it is argued, our hearts could go out to him. Consequently, Yeats quickly realized that mere revision of the play was not sufficient, and in 1907, with the help of Lady Gregory, he set about rewriting it. The 'dogmatism and rhetorical arrogance' has been swept away, and the new play, *The Unicorn from the Stars*, has for hero 'a man so plunged in trance that he could not be otherwise than all but still and silent, though perhaps with the stillness and silence of a lamp'.[31]

The Unicorn from the Stars resolves several of the dramatic difficulties of *Where There is Nothing*. The reckless advocacy of drunkenness, which was not backed by sound intellectual argument in *Where There is Nothing*, is removed from the mouth of the central character, Martin Hearne, to the mouth of a subsidiary one, his brother Andrew. Also, credibility and dramatic force are infused into the play through a clever manipulation of misunderstanding between the characters. Martin finds it easy to gather an army to destroy the world, because his followers, mistaking him for Johnny Gibbons, the exiled Irish patriot returning from France, believe that he is really gathering an army to destroy England. When Martin proclaims that he must destroy the Church, his followers believe that he means merely 'Luther's church'; when Martin proclaims that he must destroy Law, his followers believe that he means merely English Law, the law made for the profit of the English and the subjugation of the ancient Irish race. Misunderstanding between characters is an old dramatic trick, but by making it the immediate motivation for action Yeats and Lady Gregory gave credibility to the strange message they had to impart: in *Where There is Nothing* Paul's dogmatism and arrogance made it easy for the audience to reject his vision, but in *The Unicorn from the Stars* the audience are held in uneasy tension between what they know to be misinterpretation on the part of the subsidiary characters and the strangeness of a message which they are called upon to verify. Through the dramatic technique, also, a new dimension is added to the play: men can only half understand visionary truths, and it is, perhaps, only in momentary misinterpretation and illusion that they can be stirred to action by the words of the visionary.

But the chief difference between *Where There is Nothing* and *The Unicorn from the Stars* is a shift of focus from the material to the spiritual world. During the eighteen-nineties Yeats had argued that the material world must be regarded as an expression of the spiritual. Later, in *The Hour Glass*, he had explored the fate and folly of those who deny the reality of the spiritual world: the chief character of the play, a Wise Man, has taught that the only truth man can know is based on sense impressions, but when faced with the certainty of death and the sudden disintegration of his material world the Wise Man is made to realize that Heaven is denied only to those who deny the existence of Heaven, that when our bodies die our souls awaken, that 'there is a spiritual kingdom that cannot be seen or known till the faculties, whereby we master the kingdom of this world, wither away like green things in winter.'[32] *The Hour Glass* shows that there are two worlds, 'the one visible and the one invisible; and when it is winter with us it is summer in that country, and when the November winds are up among us it is lambing-time there.'[33] In other words, when the light of material sense goes out, whether with physical death or with vision (which, as Yeats argues elsewhere, is 'a kind of death'),[34] the soul returns to the spiritual kingdom which is its heritage: 'We sink in on God, we find Him in becoming nothing — we perish into reality.'[35]

In *The Hour Glass* the prospect of physical death brings the soul to the acceptance of the spiritual world it had previously denied, but in *The Unicorn from the Stars* the soul is brought into union with the spiritual world in a moment of vision or trance. During almost half of the action of the play Martin Hearne is plunged in trance and the truths revealed to him provide the motivation for the rest of the action of the play. Action in the material world must come as a consequence of the spiritual truths revealed in vision, but it must not be initiated for its material effects; it must, Martin insists, become 'the overflowing of . . . idleness,' the expression of the 'secret frenzy' of the heart.[36] Consequently in *The Unicorn from the Stars* the reckless raging violence of *Where There is Nothing* is replaced by secret joy, exultation, and ecstasy: the brazen beast has been exorcized and the unicorn becomes the dominant apocalyptic symbol:

FATHER JOHN   Tell me what you have seen, where you have been.

MARTIN   There were horses — white horses rushing by, with white shining riders — there was a horse without a rider, and some one caught me up and put me upon him and rode away, like the wind, like the wind. . . . We went on, on, on. We came to a sweet-smelling garden with a gate to it, and there were wheatfields in full ear around, and there were vineyards like I saw in France, and the grapes in bunches. I thought it to be one of the townlands of Heaven. Then I saw the horses we were on had changed to unicorns, and they began trampling the grapes and breaking them. I tried to stop them, but I could not. . . . They tore down the wheat and trampled it on stones, and then they tore down what was left of the grapes and crushed and bruised and trampled them. I smelt the wine, it was flowing on every side. . . . I saw the unicorns trampling, and then a figure, a many-changing figure, holding some bright thing. I knew something was going to happen or to be said, something that would make my whole life strong and beautiful like the rushing of the unicorns. . . .[37]

It 'is only when one has put work away', Martin maintains, 'that one begins to live.'[38] For involvement with the mundane world shuts one's 'window into eternity'.[39] But once one has achieved momentary union with the spiritual world in vision one can return to the material world filled with the energy, secret exaltation, joy, and self-sufficiency of the angels and unicorns one has seen in vision. All action then becomes an overflowing of joy and secret spiritual energy:

No man can be alive, and what is Paradise but fullness of life, if whatever he sets his hand to in the daylight cannot carry him from exaltation to exaltation, and if he does not rise into the frenzy of contemplation in the night silence. Events that are not begotten in joy are misbegotten and darken the world, and nothing is begotten in joy if the joy of a thousand years has not been crushed into a moment.[40]

Yeats planned *The Unicorn from the Stars* 'to carry to a more complete realization the central idea of the stories of *The Secret Rose*' and he believed that the play had 'more natural affinities' with those stories than with *Where There is Nothing*.[41] The central idea of *The Secret Rose* was, as we have seen, the conflict between the natural and spiritual order, between the 'outer order and outer fixity' of the material world[42] and the inner spiritual light that the human heart is capable of knowing and serving. Many of the stories of *The Secret Rose* externalize this conflict, but in *The Unicorn from the Stars* the external conflict, which had played such a central part in *Where There is Nothing*, between Paul and the materialistic magistrates, and between Paul and the orthodox Friars, has been removed. It is true that Martin leads an 'army' to bring his message into the world by physical action, but this is because he has only imperfectly understood the message, because having been drawn back from vision too quickly by his anxious family he is led to believe that a beggar with 'destruction' on his lips is a messenger from God. During the course of the play Martin is made to realize that regeneration of the individual spirit does not lie in destroying or even in converting the world, but in understanding and expressing what has been revealed in vision. To attempt to destroy the Church, Law, and the material world in a sudden cataclysmic act is, Martin recognizes at the end of the play, 'but a frenzy'. The visionary's business is 'not reformation but revelation', not the physical destruction of the external world but the piercing in a moment of vision of 'the wild heart of time.'[43] The battle between the material and spiritual, between sense and spirit, is, therefore, not external but internal, not cosmic but individual, not immediately and ultimately resolved but endless: it is fought eternally within the individual mind and can be won or lost in a moment, for in that moment all that comes between man and God is suddenly insignificant:

> I was mistaken when I set out to destroy Church and Law. The battle we have to fight is fought out in our own mind. There is a fiery moment, perhaps once in a lifetime, and in that moment

> we see the only thing that matters. It is in that moment the great battles are lost and won, for in that moment we are a part of the host of Heaven. . . . I thought the battle was here, and that the joy was to be found here on earth, that all one had to do was to bring again the old wild earth of the stories — but no, it is not here; we shall not come to that joy, that battle, till we have put out the senses, everything that can be seen and handled, as I put out this candle. . . . We must put out the whole world as I put out this candle. . . . We must put out the light of the stars and the light of the sun and the light of the moon . . . till we have brought everything to nothing once again. I saw in a broken vision, but now all is clear to me. Where there is nothing, where there is nothing — there is God!⁴⁴

Heaven is won or lost in a moment and Heaven, Martin argues, is not as it has been depicted traditionally, but there the qualities which are unique to each individual are brought to fruition:

> Heaven is not what we have believed it to be. It is not quiet, it is not singing and making music, and all strife at an end. I have seen it, I have been there. The lover still loves, but with a greater passion, and the rider still rides, but the horse goes like the wind and leaps the ridges, and the battle goes on always, always. That is the joy of Heaven, continual battle.⁴⁵

Until the supreme act is possible, until the body and the material world are dramatically cast off in the grave, man must oscillate between the life of vision and the death of material life. Until the supreme act is possible, man 'must labour through many lives and many deaths.'⁴⁶ For while mortal breath remains man must return from vision to the material world to which for a moment he has become indifferent. Life, therefore, becomes an endless oscillation between the spiritual and material, and death becomes the supreme consummation of the ecstatic process.

The Unicorn from the Stars establishes the relationship between the spiritual and the material in clearer perspective than any of the works we have analyzed previously. We think of the movement of 'The Second Coming' where the individual, caught in the darkness of material life, apprehends in a moment of vision the character of the new dispensation, and returns after the moment of vision to the darkness into which he and the material world are plunged at the beginning of the poem. This movement and balance is integral also to the structure of many of Yeats's plays, as the spiritual image at the core of each play is bounded at beginning and end by material concerns. The juxtaposition of the material and spiritual in this way, the juxtaposition of incongruities, one of which is as essential as the other, leads, of course, to the absurd.

We have traced Yeats's progression of symbols to this point: twilight, the rose, the wind among the reeds, the brazen beast, the trampling unicorns. In *The Unicorn from the Stars* we have the emergence of a new symbol, the symbol which dominates his work during the early part of the twentieth century, the agate lamp, the stillness and silence of an individual as his soul burns with illumination and vision.

EPILOGUE

Chiefly under the influence of Synge, in whom Yeats could see a living embodiment of the philosophical principles he was discovering in Nietzsche, Yeats's thought, at the beginning of the twentieth century, enters a new phase. The aesthetic basis for this change is expounded in *Samhain*, the organ of the Irish Dramatic Movement, and in the essays later collected in *The Cutting of An Agate*.

The scientific movement, Yeats argues in these essays, had pushed literature into one of two directions: into subservience to an external reality or a concern with rarefied essences. One type was concerned with the spiritual element that the other literature denied, but denied the interest in common life with which the other literature was too closely concerned. Yeats, as we have seen, was preoccupied with rarefied essences during the eighteen-nineties; during the first part of the twentieth century, however, Synge restored for him the balance between art and life, the spiritual and the common.

In Synge's discovery of an objective correlative in the life and language of the west of Ireland, of a concrete way of making a personal emotion objective and dramatic, Yeats found a perfect example of the type of synchronization possible between an artist's mood and the external experiences he presents in his work: he 'was a drifting silent man', Yeats writes, 'and loved wild islands, because there, set out in the light of day, he saw what lay hidden in himself.'[1] As a consequence, too, of Synge's ability to present imaginative richness side by side with the naked realities of material existence, all 'that stings into life the sense of tragedy',[2] Yeats turns from the literature of impossible purities to the literature of *personality*, a literature that emanates not merely from the brain, imagination, or sensations, but from *the whole man*, of 'blood, imagination, intellect, running together'.[3] Symbolism had become associated in his mind with an unreal spiritual art; consequently he supplants it with the concept of personality, a concern with the living essence that animates individual thought and action, whether in life or literature. 'I have always come to this certainty', Yeats writes in 1906, 'what moves natural men in the arts is what moves them in life, and that is, intensity of personal life, intonations that show them, in a book or a play, the strength, the essential moment of a man who would be exciting in the market or at the dispensary door.'[4] Personality is the expression, without regard to circumstance or accruing advantage, of the energy that is unique to an individual expressing himself in active life or in passionate feeling.

With Synge too Yeats no longer had to look to ancient legend or beyond the manifest world for his apocalyptic symbols. There, in his own country and in his own theatre was the living embodiment of all he was struggling to create, a symbol that embodied the aesthetic and apocalyptic qualities he had been emphasizing: strength, self-sufficiency, laughter, the union of contraries, all the qualities later embodied in Yeats's great apocalyptic symbol, the 'shape with lion body and the head of a man' in 'The Second Coming', the uncompromising combination of instinct and intellect, of overflowing turbulent energy and brooding intellectual silence. *Where There is Nothing* had emphasized the raging violence of the apocalyptic agent, but with the example of Synge before him Yeats emphasizes joy, exaltation, ecstasy, the expression and realization of personality, the thinking of the body as well as the ideals of the mind.

NOTES

I : THE NATURE OF SYMBOLISM

1. C. Maurice Bowra, *Memories* (London 1966), pp. 240-1.
2. *The Letters of W. B. Yeats*, ed. Allan Wade (London 1954), p. 592.
3. Lecture delivered on 9 March 1910. My italics. Manuscript in the possession of Senator Michael Yeats.
4. *Savoy* (July 1896), p. 41. This passage was omitted when the essay was published in *Ideas of Good and Evil*.
5. For general analyses of symbolism see C. M. Bowra, *The Heritage of Symbolism* (London 1943); Edmund Wilson, *Axel's Castle* (New York and London 1947); A. G. Lehmann, *The Symbolic Aesthetic in France, 1885-1895* (Oxford 1968); Northrop Frye, *Anatomy of Criticism* (Princeton 1957), pp. 71-128. For specific analyses of Yeats's symbolism see *The Permanence of Yeats*, ed. James Hall and Martin Steinmann (New York 1950), pp. 264-77; Richard Ellmann, *The Identity of Yeats* (London 1954), pp. 24-38, 62-84, 146-79, 245-6; Frank Kermode, *The Romantic Image* (London 1957), pp. 107-18; Georgio Melchiori, *The Whole Mystery of Art* (London 1960), pp. 14-34; T. R. Henn, 'Yeats's Symbolism', in *The Integrity of Yeats*, ed. Denis Donoghue (Cork 1964), pp. 33-46; Leonard Nathan, *The Tragic Drama of William Butler Yeats* (New York and London 1965), pp. 50-64; Thomas Parkinson, *W. B. Yeats: The Later Poetry* (Berkeley and Los Angeles 1964), pp. 114-80; Edward Engelberg, *The Vast Design: Patterns in W. B. Yeats's Aesthetic* (Toronto 1964), pp. 63-5, 96-116, 120-2; Dwight Eddins, *Yeats: The Nineteenth Century Matrix* (Alabama 1971), pp. 128-54.
6. Ellis kept few of his own manuscripts but carefully preserved the manuscript of the section of the work for which Yeats was responsible. The Yeats manuscript was acquired for the University of Reading by Ian Fletcher and D. J. Gordon some time ago, and a book, *Blake, Ellis, and Yeats*, which is based on the 250-page manuscript, is being prepared for publication.
7. See *Letters*, p. 170, and also the Yeats manuscripts at the University of Reading.
8. *Essays and Introductions* (London 1961), p. 111.
9. *The Works of William Blake*, 3 vols. (London 1893), I, 236.
10. *Ibid.*, p. 237.
11. *Ibid.*, pp. 239-40. Yeats is of course following Swedenborg here, but the question of influences has not been explored in this study.
12. *Ibid.*, p. 241.
13. *Ibid.*, pp. 241-2.
14. *Letters*, p. 607.
15. *Works of Blake*, I, 327-8.

16 *Ibid.*, p. 315.
17 *Essays and Introductions*, p. 117.
18 *Letters*, p. 261.
19 *Essays and Introductions*, p. 18.
20 *Ibid.*, p. 154.
21 *Ibid.*, pp. 79-80.
22 *The Celtic Twilight* (London 1893), p. 6.
23 *Essays and Introductions*, p. 28.
24 *Ibid.*, p. 148.
25 *Ibid.*, p. 156.
26 *Ibid.*, p. 367.
27 *Ibid.*, p. 148.
28 *Ibid.*, p. 147.
29 *Ibid.*, p. 116.
30 *Works of Blake*, I, p. 307.
31 *Ibid.*, p. 291.
32 *Ibid.*, pp. 291-2. See also pp. 310-1.
33 *Essays and Introductions*, p. 171.
34 *Ibid.*, pp. 192-3.
35 *Ibid.*, p. 195.
36 *Ibid.*, pp. 201-2.
37 *Ibid.*, pp. 195-6.
38 *Ibid.*, p. 194.
39 *Ibid.*, p. 112.
40 *Ibid.*, pp. 163-4.
41 *Ibid.*, p. 190.
42 Manuscript of *The Works of William Blake*, University of Reading Library.
43 *Letters*, p. 211.

II : TWILIGHT AND THE ROSE

1 *Essays and Introductions*, p. 114. See also pp. 149-50.
2 *The Secret Rose* (London 1897), pp. 142-3.
3 *Mythologies* (London 1961), p. 98. I shall quote from this edition of the work, except when a different version of a particular story appears in an earlier edition, and when the earlier version is significant for my argument. For Yeats's revisions in *The Celtic Twilight* see Richard J. Finneran, 'Yeats's Revisions in *The Celtic Twilight*, 1912-1925', *Tulane Studies in English*, 20 (1972), 97-105.
4 *The Celtic Twilight* (London 1893), p. 140.
5 *Ideals in Ireland*, ed. Augusta Gregory (London 1901), p. 101.
6 *Fairy and Folk Tales of the Irish Peasantry* (London 1888), p. xii.
7 *Essays and Introductions*, p. 41.
8 Augusta Gregory, *Gods and Fighting Men* (London 1904), p. xii.

9   *Mythologies*, p. 104.
10 *Essays and Introductions*, p. 42.
11 Ibid., p. 181 and p. 179.
12 *The Celtic Twilight* (1893), p. 25.
13 Ibid., p. 199.
14 *Essays and Introductions*, p. 6.
15 *Mythologies*, p. 80.
16 *Essays and Introductions*, p. 182.
17 Ibid.
18 *The Celtic Twilight* (1893), pp. 24-5 and p. 20.
19 *Mythologies*, p. 30.
20 *The Celtic Twilight* (1893), pp. 6-7.
21 *Mythologies*, p. 139.
22 *Essays and Introductions*, p. 11.
23 Unpublished Yeats Lecture (1903). Manuscript in the possession of Senator Michael Yeats.
24 *Collected Poems*, p. 51.
25 *Mythologies*, pp. 138-9.
26 *The Secret Rose* (1897), pp. 2-4. For other critical treatments of *The Secret Rose* see Richard J. Finneran, *The Prose Fiction of W. B. Yeats: The Search for 'Those Simple Forms'* (Dublin 1973); Augustine Martin, '"The Secret Rose" and Yeats's Dialogue with History', *Ariel*, 3, No. 3 (July 1972); Phillip L. Marcus, *Yeats and the Beginning of the Irish Renaissance* (Cornell 1970), pp. 35-60.
27 Ibid., p. 9.
28 *Mythologies*, p. 201.
29 Ibid., p. 210.
30 *The Secret Rose* (1897), p. 199.
31 Ibid., p. 44.
32 *Mythologies*, pp. 151-2.
33 Ibid., p. 149.
34 Yeats reviewed Meyer's edition of the tale in *The Bookman* (February 1893). See John P. Frayne, *Uncollected Prose of W. B. Yeats* (London 1970), pp. 261-3. See also *Letters*, p. 285.
35 *Mythologies*, p. 155.
36 Ibid., p. 178.
37 Ibid., p. 68.
38 Ibid., p. 189.
39 Ibid., p. 173.
40 Ibid., p. 173 and p. 171.
41 Ibid., p. 172.
42 Ibid., pp. 162-3.
43 Ibid., pp. 168-9.
44 Ibid., p. 170.

45 For the different versions of the Hanrahan stories see *Yeats Studies: An International Journal* (Dublin 1971), pp. 119-74. Because I am concerned in this chapter with Yeats's thought during the latter part of the eighteen-nineties, I have quoted from *The Secret Rose* version of the stories. For another critical treatment of the Hanrahan stories see Richard J. Finneran, ' "Old lecher with a love on every wind": A Study of Yeats's Stories of Red Hanrahan', *Texas Studies in Language and Literature*, 14, No. 2 (1972), 347-58.
46 *Mythologies*, p. 220.
47 Ibid., p. 221.
48 Ibid., p. 233.
49 *The Secret Rose* (1897), pp. 137-8.
50 Ibid., pp. 138-9.
51 Ibid., p. 139.
52 Ibid., p. 183.
53 Ibid., p. 149.
54 Ibid., p. 154. My italics.
55 Ibid., pp. 143-4.
56 Ibid., pp. 181-2.
57 Ibid., p. 189.
58 Ibid., p. 196.
59 *Collected Poems*, pp. 221-2.

III : FROM DREAM TO VISION
1 *Mythologies*, p. 268.
2 Ibid., p. 267.
3 Ibid., p. 270.
4 Ibid., p. 269.
5 *Variorum Poems* (London 1957), p. 808.
6 *Mythologies*, p. 273.
7 Ibid., p. 285.
8 *Savoy* (April 1896), pp. 66-7.
9 *Mythologies*, p. 276.
10 Ibid., pp. 274-5.
11 Ibid., p. 282.
12 Ibid., p. 287.
13 Ibid., p. 280.
14 Yeats used this word in the first version of the story in the *Savoy*, but changed it to 'magnetic' in *The Secret Rose* version in 1897.
15 *Mythologies*, p. 277.
16 Ibid., p. 280.
17 Ibid., p. 286.
18 Ibid., p. 287 and p. 290.
19 Ibid., p. 278.

20 *Ibid.*, p. 292.
21 All quotations from *The Tables of the Law* are taken from 'The Tables of the Law: A Critical Text', *Yeats Studies* (1971), pp. 102-18. This quotation occurs on p. 104.
22 *Yeats Studies* (1971), p. 103.
23 *Collected Poems*, p. 182.
24 *Yeats Studies* (1971), p. 106.
25 Joyce, according to Richard Ellmann, knew *The Tables of the Law* by heart (*Eminent Domain: Yeats among Wilde, Joyce, Pound, Eliot and Auden* (New York 1967), p. 42).
26 *Yeats Studies* (1971), p. 111.
27 *Ibid.*, p. 110.
28 *Ibid.*, p. 111.
29 *Ibid.*, p. 116.
30 *Ibid.*, p. 112.
31 *Ibid.*, p. 116.
32 *Ibid.*
33 *Autobiographies*, p. 314.
34 *Dublin Daily Express*, 27 August 1898. Reprinted in Rolleston and Brooke, *A Treasury of Irish Poetry* (London 1900), pp. 465-7, and in Volume VIII of the *Collected Works* in 1908, pp. 183-8.
35 *Mythologies*, p. 309.
36 *Ibid.*, p. 312.
37 *Ibid.*
38 *Ibid.*, pp. 313-4.
39 *Ibid.*, p. 307.
40 *Ibid.*, p. 278.
41 *Ibid.*, p. 315.
42 *Variorum Poems*, p. 852.

IV : SOME IMPLICATIONS OF THE SYMBOLIC APPROACH

1 *Essays and Introductions*, p. 53.
2 *Ibid.*, p. 150.
3 *Ibid.*, p. 47.
4 *Ibid.*, p. 53.
5 For previous analyses of *The Wind Among the Reeds* see Forrest Reid, *W. B. Yeats: A Critical Study* (London 1915), pp. 64-91; Bowra, *The Heritage of Symbolism*, pp. 188-93; John Unterecker, *A Reader's Guide to William Butler Yeats* (New York 1959), pp. 87-95; A. G. Stock, *W. B. Yeats: His Poetry and Thought* (Cambridge 1961), pp. 37-54; A. Norman Jeffares, *A Commentary on the Collected Poems of W. B. Yeats* (London 1968), pp. 48-85; Allan Grossman, *Poetic Knowledge in the Early Yeats: A Study of The Wind Among The Reeds* (Virginia 1969); Eddins, *Yeats*, pp. 108-27; Harold Bloom, *Yeats* (New York 1970), pp. 121-32.

6   *Variorum Poems*, p. 806.
7   *The Bookman*, April 1894. See Frayne, *Uncollected Prose*, p. 324.
8   *The Celtic Twilight* (1893), p. 18.
9   *Collected Poems*, p. 37.
10 *Mythologies*, p. 104.
11 *Collected Poems*, p. 35. Unless otherwise specified, all quotations are taken from the *Collected Poems*.
12 *Variorum Poems*, p. 842.
13 'Intellectual Beauty has not only the happy dead to do her will, but ministering spirits who correspond to the Devas of the East, and the Elemental Spirits of medieval Europe, and the Sidhe of ancient Ireland' (*Essays and Introductions*, p. 74).
14 *Collected Poems*, p. 232.
15 The last two lines were written in 1922 and replaced

> Although the rushes and the fowl of the air
> Cry of his love with their pitiful cries.

of the earlier versions.
16 *Variorum Poems*, p. 843.
17 *Mythologies*, p. 100.
18 *The Wind among the Reeds* (1899), p. 51.
19 *Essays and Introductions*, p. 88. So also p. 133, where Yeats writes, 'Dante, like other medieval writers, symbolized the highest order of created beings by the fixed stars, and God by the darkness beyond them, the *Primum Mobile*.'
20 *The Prophecies of SS. Columbkille* (Dublin 1856), p. 8.
21 Notes to *Congal* (Dublin and London 1872), p. 212. Ferguson incorporates the myth into his poem :

>   the King himself he found
> With gathered Erin in his tents, fast camped, beside the fosse
> That in the magic days of old the Black Boar scooped across
> Orgallia's border : he who now, from dry land banished far,
> No longer casts up rampart dykes to stem the tide of war,
> But rooting round the island rocks where Brecan's cauldrons boil,
> Turns up the ridgy-rolling sea with ever-fruitless toil;
> For fast as still with furrowing tusk he grooves the wave, so fast
> The fluent-rising wave forbids to champ the illusive mast.
>   (*Congal*, p. 52)

22 'The Folklore of the Black Pig's Dyke', *Ulster Folk Life*, II (1957), 30-1.
23 *The Irish Times*, 1 May 1918.
24 *Mythologies*, p. 111.
25 *Variorum Poems*, p. 843.
26 *Ibid.*, p. 807.
27 *Ibid.*, p. 161.

28 *Ibid.*, p. 808.
29 *Ibid.*, p. 807.
30 *Essays and Introductions*, p. 90.
31 *Variorum Poems*, p. 809.
32 *Ibid.*, p. 810.
33 *Ibid.*
34 *Ibid.*
35 *Mythologies*, p. 281.

V : A BEAST AND A UNICORN

1   *Variorum Plays* (London 1966), p. 1145.
2   *Ibid.*, p. 1071.
3   *Ibid.*, pp. 1098-9.
4   *Ibid.*, p. 1140.
5   *Ibid.*, p. 1157.
6   *Ibid.*, p. 932.
7   *Essays and Introductions*, p. 322.
8   *Letters*, p. 406.
9   *Variorum Plays*, p. 1072 and p. 1071.
10 *Ibid.*, p. 1082.
11 *Ibid.*, p. 1081.
12 *Ibid.*, p. 1097.
13 *Ibid.*, p. 1132.
14 *Mythologies*, p. 312.
15 *Collected Plays*, p. 338.
16 *Variorum Plays*, p. 1125.
17 *Ibid.*, p. 1147.
18 *Ibid.*, p. 1132 and p. 1133.
19 *Ibid.*, pp. 1137-9.
20 *Ibid.*, p. 1084.
21 *Ibid.*, p. 1137.
22 *Ibid.*, pp. 1139-40.
23 *Ibid.*, p. 1147.
24 *Ibid.*, pp. 1157-8.
25 *Ibid.*, p. 1158.
26 *Ibid.*, p. 1153.
27 *Ibid.*, p. 1160.
28 This, of course, is Yeats's version of the story. Lady Gregory and Douglas Hyde helped him to write the play. As a consequence, when we quote from the play and from its rewritten version, *The Unicorn from the Stars*, we are not even sure that we are quoting Yeats's words, for although he could recognize in the play 'thoughts, a point of view, an artistic aim which seem a part of my world', the 'handiwork', he admits, was almost wholly Lady Gregory's (*Variorum Plays*, p. 712).

29 *Variorum Plays*, p. 1296.
30 *Ibid.*, p. 712.
31 *Ibid.*
32 *Ibid.*, p. 585.
33 *Ibid.*, p. 578.
34 *Essays and Introductions*, p. 71.
35 *Variorum Plays*, p. 634.
36 *Collected Plays*, p. 362.
37 *Ibid.*, pp. 337-44.
38 *Ibid.*, p. 362.
39 *Ibid.*, p. 343.
40 *Ibid.*, p. 362.
41 *Letters*, p. 503.
42 *Mythologies*, p. 162.
43 *Collected Plays*, p. 378 and p. 377.
44 *Ibid.*, pp. 378-82.
45 *Ibid.*, p. 381.
46 *Essays and Introductions*, p. 137.

EPILOGUE

1 *Essays and Introductions*, p. 330.
2 *Ibid.*, p. 327.
3 *Ibid.*, p. 266.
4 *Ibid.*, p. 265.